GETTING THE BEST OF YOUR
DISSERTATION

BY DAVE HARRIS

Portland, OR

Some of the most exhilarating experiences we undergo are generated inside the mind, triggered by information that challenges our ability to think . . . As Sir Francis Bacon noted . . . wonder—which is the seed of knowledge—is the reflection of the purest form of pleasure.

— Mihalyi Csikszentmihalyi, *Flow*, 1990

"Philosophy" (n.):
From Greek *philosophia* meaning love (*philia*) of wisdom (*sophia*).

"Ph.D.":
Standard abbreviation for the title "Doctor of Philosophy"

FORWARD

Doctoral dissertations are difficult, but the difficulties are not the whole story. You can get a lot of benefit from writing a dissertation—more than just the benefit of getting your degree and finishing your doctoral program.

What does the dissertation offer?

- For starters, there is the obvious benefit of getting the degree you've been seeking, which includes being able to pursue goals. Along with that, you get to stop paying fees to your school.

- Beyond that, the dissertation—like many challenges—can be a wonderful learning experience: doing difficult things isn't necessarily bad—we can soften Nietzsche's famed dictum into the following pair of ideas: "that which challenges us may make us stronger; that which does not won't."

- Additionally, the dissertation is often a foundation for later publication. Publication is obviously valuable for those planning a career in publish-or-perish academia, but can benefit professionals, too.

- And most importantly, challenging projects that involve intellectual development can be interesting and fun, even when faced with frustration—there is, after all, a reason that "philosophy" has an etymological basis as "love of wisdom."

Writing a dissertation is not easy, but there is good reason to believe that, "The best moments [in our lives] usually occur when a person's body or mind is stretched to its limits in a voluntary effort to accomplish something difficult and worthwhile" (Csikszentmihalyi, p. 3).

For over a decade, I have helped dissertation writers who are stuck and struggling—with their material, with their committee, and with themselves and their own self-confidence. In that time, I have found that if you look at the issues in the right way, the worst difficulties can be overcome much more easily, and you can even find a lot to like.

This book presents perspectives on the dissertation project that will help you work more effectively and with a greater sense of reward in your work. From the importance of living well, to the purposes of research and the corresponding influence on research methods, to practical issues in managing a project, this book contains ideas I have used to help writers work more effectively, work successfully with their faculty committee, and, finally, finish.

These principles are not obscure. Some are so obvious that they are taken for granted, and thus left out of consideration when planning. Others seem counter-intuitive when approached from the wrong angle. Sometimes we do not see or understand the whole forest because our attention is focused on the specific trees that surround us.

I believe that if you look at the dissertation in the right way, you can complete it successfully, and you can benefit greatly from the challenge. The dissertation is supposed to be an opportunity for growth of skill and understanding. It is a learning experience that can provide a foundation for a successful, rewarding career in a field where sophisticated knowledge is crucial—whether academic or professional. The dissertation should be a challenge; it should take you beyond your previous experience into places where you are challenged to grow. The dissertation need not be an ordeal that you struggle to survive. If you use the right perspectives, it won't be.

Whether you are pursuing an academic career or a professional one, I'll bet you had real interest in the field you chose. The dissertation is an opportunity to develop your knowledge and understanding of that field. And, like any true challenge, it is an opportunity to understand yourself better, too. Finishing a dissertation can be a great experience. It can absolutely be worth the time, effort, and expense.

By looking at it from the right perspectives, you can get the best your dissertation has to offer.

CONTENTS

ANNOTATED
TABLE OF CONTENTS

1: ABOUT THIS BOOK

Dissertations are difficult, but they're not without rewards. By taking a moment to step back to get different views of your task, you can approach it more productively. Like the artist who steps back from the easel, you can benefit from stepping back to get a different perspective on your project. This book presents several different perspectives on the dissertation so that you can get the best the dissertation has to offer.

2: PERSPECTIVES ON THE DISSERTATION

Despite the horror stories that surround them, and the true difficulties they present, dissertations are not intended to make students suffer, and looking at dissertations that way doesn't provide much guidance for effective action. There are realistic perspectives on the dissertation that do provide effective guidance. These perspectives are no mystery, though they are the kind of idea that people take for granted due to familiarity. Effective action is guided by seeing and understanding what the dissertation does expect: that you express your own idea, derived from your own research. The richer and clearer your view of the process, the more effective your efforts. Whatever the situation or difficulty, a good perspective will help guide effective action, but sometimes finding the most useful perspective requires stepping back from the project to consider all the different angles.

3: LIVING WELL

The most important perspectives to consider are those that motivate the work: Why are you doing it at all? What are the larger life goals that motivated entering a doctoral program? What purposes does the dissertation serve? How will it serve them? And what are the sacrifices you must make to achieve these ends? Has the dissertation become a battle for survival? Can you finish your dissertation without ruining your life? Plan as if the dissertation is meant to support your life; don't plan as if it requires you to sacrifice your life.

3.1: LIVING A BETTER LIFE

What are your life goals? If you're like most dissertation writers, you have a larger purpose in mind; you're not just aiming to write a dissertation. Whether you plan an academic or professional career, by keeping long-term priorities in mind, you will make better decisions than you would if focused only on more immediate demands. By keeping long-term priorities in mind, you can develop a healthy relationship with your dissertation instead of letting it take over your life.

3.2: PRACTICE AND DEVELOPMENT OF SKILLS

Whatever your larger goals, you serve them by developing a regular practice that develops your skills and abilities. When you work on research, you call into action many abilities that will be refined and honed as you work. The more you practice, the better your general ability, and the better your general ability, the easier it is to deal with any task.

3.3: REGULAR PRACTICE AND MOMENTUM

One of the easiest ways to make any task easier is to practice regularly and build momentum in your practice. By working regularly—every day or almost every day—you build rhythms that support work, and you don't have to spend time "getting back up to speed" on a project you haven't seen for a week. It's not easy to build up momentum on a project, but the overall effort expended is reduced if you gather momentum and keep moving.

3.4: THE BEST THINGS IN LIFE

The dissertation can be a positive experience, but even if everything goes exactly according to plan, there's a lot of work required, as well as a significant commitment of time and money. What are you going to get from the dissertation? And what are the costs will you pay to get those things? If you see all the opportunities for benefit, and you can plan effectively to minimize costs, you are likely to get the best your dissertation has to offer.

4: A PROJECT TO BE COMPLETED

Shifting our view from your life as a whole in which the dissertation is part, to looking at the dissertation as a task to be carried out, we first consdier the dissertation as a large project that you have to manage and bring to completion. From this perspective we can apply insights about conditions faced by those managing similar projects.

5: RESEARCH

The next perspective of interest looks at research. There are a number of perspectives from philosophy of science and epistemology that provide guidance for practical action in research. There is a gap between the idealized search for truth and the practical issues of research, and often it takes some re-imagining of the nature and process of research to move from being a student consuming the research of others to being the creator of your own research.

5.1: A STORY ABOUT HOW THE WORLD WORKS

At its heart, research is an attempt to understand and explain. It is an attempt to tell a story of how the world works—but not just any explanation or story will do. Research is the generation of explanations of various phenomena—stories about how things in the world behave—using methods accepted by the academic community of which you are part. The conventions of research can obscure the process of telling an explanatory story, but ultimately, all research is aimed at the creation of such stories.

5.2: RESEARCH QUESTIONS 1: RESEARCH INTERESTS AND THE WEB OF QUESTIONS

Research is driven by curiosity about some story about the world. Initial motivation typically comes from a general sense that the story currently told in the research community needs to be refined—that there is some gap or error in the story. This story is the context in which you define and refine a more precise research question that addresses the question—the gap or the error—that motivated the project.

5.3: A MANAGEABLE QUESTION

In order to bring research projects to completion, the crucial step is to identify a research question that defines a manageable project. No matter how crucial or interesting your question, if it doesn't lead to a completed project, it doesn't help you or anyone else. Setting practical limits for a small project is more effective and more valuable than pursuing some grand project that will never be completed.

5.4: THE LARGER RESEARCH DISCOURSE

So far, I have spoken of research from an individual point of view: the attempt of an individual scholar to define a research project that helps explain the world. But research is a community activity concerned not only with the discovery of understanding, but with its dissemination as well. As a researcher, all your work is done within a web of ideas built up within a research community. Understanding how to place your work in that web is crucial to the effective use of literature and the effective definition of a research question.

6: WRITING

A dissertation project is not just the generation of original research, it is the written expression of that research. The demands of writing differ from the demands of research, and being able to see the writing as writing—an attempt to communicate ideas to other people—provides practical guidance.

6.1: A PIECE OF WRITING

One concern for the writer is with the form of the written work to be created: what makes up a dissertation? And how can be it be done so that it is well received? When one thinks of writing in terms of the attempt to be heard and understood, many of the issues that frustrate writers—punctuation, grammar, structure—make more sense. If your goal is to get your dissertation accepted and completed, your task is facilitated by having a clear sense of how to write so that you meet your audience's expectations.

6.2: COMPLETING WRITING PROJECTS

In addition to thinking about the forms that help you reach readers, there are also the concerns of how to set up a writing practice and the management of a writing project. Managing a dissertation-length work is a significant undertaking. Good practices will facilitate your efforts.

7: INSTITUTIONAL ACCEPTANCE

Another crucial perspective is that of the dissertation's place in the institution: if dissertations are not simply a rite of passage or some device to torture you before you receive your degree, then what are they for? Issues of research and writing—the discovery and communication of ideas—do not explain why the university asks students to write dissertations, nor do they give any guidance for dealing with individuals within the institution whose intentions might not be entirely benevolent.

7.1: A TEST OF YOUR ABILITY

The dissertation is a test of your ability—the final test given by universities before granting doctoral degrees—and it is also an exercise meant to develop skills and abilities. So what skills and abilities is it supposed to develop and test? The better you understand what the university is looking for, the better you can get the developmental benefit the project is intended to have, and the more easily you can fulfill the desires and expectations of the university's representatives—your professors or reviewers.

7.2: MANAGING PROFESSORS

In practical terms, the institution manifests in the person of the professors (and perhaps other faculty/staff) who review your work. Therefore, central to fulfilling the institutional requirements is to fulfill the desires and expectations of those with whom you work and those who will review your work. Speaking pragmatically, and perhaps a bit cynically, you will benefit from thinking about what you want to get and how you can get it from the people with whom you work.

CONCLUSION

Ultimately, I believe that almost everybody who has started a dissertation will be best served by finishing the dissertation as soon as possible and then getting on with the rest of their life. By closing the door on your dissertation—even if it is imperfect—you will open new doors, doors that you may have been aiming at for years! So step back from the task for a moment. Take the time to look at it from different angles, and make some plans for effective action to bring it all to a beneficial conclusion.

CHAPTER 1:
ABOUT THIS BOOK

Dissertations are difficult, but they're not without rewards. By taking a moment to step back to get different views of your task, you can approach it more productively. Like the artist who steps back from the easel, you can benefit from stepping back to get a different perspective on your project. This book presents several different perspectives on the dissertation to help you get the best the dissertation has to offer.

THIS BOOK IS FOR ANYONE WRITING A DISSERTATION

This book is written for anyone who would prefer to have a good experience writing their dissertation, despite the necessary work, rather than an ordeal.

Whether you are looking forward to an academic career or you are planning to escape academia as quickly as you possibly can, this book is for you.

Whether you are in the sciences or the humanities, the descriptions and ideas presented herein will suit your work.

Although I refer to doctoral dissertations throughout, this book is also suitable for master's students or undergraduates writing theses.

This book is concerned with the generation of a major research project, from conception to final presentation as a completed and accepted work. As such, its focus is on matters that are general and common, and, therefore, often familiar. In many cases, the ideas may even be obvious, but we all sometimes lose sight of, or take for granted, things we know. And sometimes old, familiar ideas can take on new importance or meaning when presented from an appropriate perspective.

In this book, I share perspectives on the dissertation that will help you understand the work that lies before you so you can work more effectively and efficiently.

This is not a recipe book or a guidebook; there is no algorithm for writing a dissertation. This is a book of principles to guide practical and effective work processes that can help you get going and keep going when things get difficult.

For academics and professionals

I often use the word "scholar" to refer to dissertation writers. Whether you plan an academic career or a professional one, if your field requires an advanced degree, then you're entering a field where you have to be at least partly a "scholar," in the sense that you have to be able to understand and judge between numerous competing theories—the clinical psychologist choosing a therapeutic method and the administrator choosing a management plan are both operating in a scholarly mode for a time. If you do not currently view yourself as a scholar, try the title on for a while. You don't have to be a scholar all the time, but for the dissertation embrace the role.

Disclaimer

Different people have different strengths and weaknesses, and different people are at different stages in their research, and so they face different problems. In trying to cover a wide range of problems faced by dissertation writers, parts of this book will be less relevant than others to any given individual. If your writing is great but you're struggling with your faculty, you may not find the material on writing very useful, for example. Or if you've got a strong understanding of theory and research in your field but you're having trouble writing, you may not need the section on research. Nonetheless, I encourage at least skimming all the sections, because a holistic view is valuable. I have attempted to keep the book short enough that it can be read quickly.

THE DISSERTATION IS NOT A PUNISHMENT

There are books that talk about how to "survive" your dissertation, as if the dissertation were some life-threatening ordeal. One dissertation book—

one that I love to hate, and so will not mention by name, nor directly quote—observes that people who have successfully finished their dissertation are often highly appreciative of their faculty committee. This seems perfectly reasonable: people who succeed are often appreciative of those who aided the success, and some professors are really helpful, wonderful people who work really hard to help their students. The book I love to hate, however, likens this appreciation to the effect of Stockholm Syndrome, in which hostages come to sympathize with their captors. To me this seems worse than silly: what benefit is gained by looking at your professors as kidnappers or torturers? What sort of pragmatic action does such an idea suggest?

Dissertations are hard. They're large and complex, and they take a lot of work. All sorts of things can go wrong, calling for more effort and more time. And that's all assuming that your professors are neither malicious nor sadistic, but rather honestly want to help.

Problems will arise, but looking for problems is not the place to start. One way that a dissertation can become an ordeal is to set out expecting the worst. If you expect to suffer, you won't think there's a problem when you are suffering, and you might not take action to avoid the suffering. Yes, dissertations are hard work, but that doesn't mean there's no good in it.

There's a saying: "if it was fun, it wouldn't be work." If you hold that attitude, then you're more likely to neglect the cues that would lead you to a place of interest, and thereby end up in a place of drudgery. The idea that work is not enjoyable, and never will be, is simply wrong. Many people work very hard, make tremendous sacrifices for their work, and love it and feel it worth all their investment.

Research has its moments of drudgery, but whether you're starting a research career or you're researching to get a professional credential, the dissertation project is an opportunity to gain insight into issues central to your anticipated career—a career that hopefully promises to be interesting.

Thinking about the dissertation as an ordeal does not give you much insight into how to work more effectively. Again, what strategy for action arises from viewing your professors as torturers? You can't call the police because your professor gave you bad feedback or told you to do a lot of work that you deem unnecessary.[1]

Dissertations are not intended to torture students. Dissertations are assigned both as a learning experience—the experience of designing, managing, and completing your own independent research project—and as a test of your ability to design, manage, and complete your own research project. Yes, dissertations are supposed to be difficult, but the difficulty is supposed to be ultimately beneficial. Taking this view of dissertations does lead to useful strategies for action. Most of the rest of this book will be dedicated to looking at pragmatic approaches suggested by looking at dissertations from a variety of perspectives.

THE DESPAIR OF THE MEANINGLESS

The psychiatrist Viktor Frankl believed that psychological disorders can arise from the sense that life, or something in life, is meaningless. He argued that people's main need is to see meaning in their life, that this need for meaning is the primary motivator in life, and that people are willing to suffer for a meaningful cause (Frankl, 1984, pp. 121, 136).

Looking at the dissertation as an ordeal can have a negative effect: it can depress your mood. If you think that the dissertation is only to make you suffer, then it has little other meaning than the suffering. If you think the ivory tower of academia has no connection with the real world, then a dissertation may feel meaningless for being disconnected from the real world. Writing a dissertation takes hard work, and hard work sometimes involves some degree of suffering—bleary eyes from reading too long, or an aching back from sitting, for example. If your back aches after a task that you thought important and interesting, you will feel very different than if your back aches after working through some task that you perceive as worthless that was assigned by a professor.

---

1 Problems that justify calling the police, or at least justify the intervention of the administration—and these do, unfortunately, exist—are outside the scope of this book. I do not make light of such things, but if you feel that one of your professors has broken a law or university policy, you need to consult someone with legal expertise.

For many dissertation writers, significant difficulty comes from seeing many dissertation tasks as meaningless—as no more than a process of jumping through the right hoops—no more than the conventional steps of some arcane rite of passage. Such views are common enough that most doctoral candidates have heard that "Ph.D." stands for "Piled Higher and Deeper." It's pretty hard to feel good about your writing and research if you think it's all just manure piled higher and deeper.

As previously noted, some people think their professors are out to torture them. I've often heard or read of professors who allegedly believe their students should suffer like they did when they were students. If you think that you are working for someone who is making you suffer to match their suffering, then the difficulty of the dissertation is compounded with frustration from believing that your efforts serve no useful purpose. I have no personal experience with professors who are actively sadistic, but I imagine there are some. In my experience, most of the horror stories I've heard centered on professors too egotistical to bother with actively hurting students. The bad professors I've known have mostly hurt students by lack of attention—by giving no feedback, by giving poor feedback, or by making suggestions based on a poor understanding of the project. One extreme case I heard of was the professor who didn't show up for a qualifying exam without notifying anyone, thus invalidating the exam. Of course, it's cold comfort to think that you're being neglected rather than tortured. Neglect can also make your efforts feel meaningless.

Other scholars worry that their work is meaningless because its scope too small, its method too fraught with limitations, the focus too insular to have meaning to many, or even because of a sense that the "ivory tower" is out of touch with the real world. Many or most people who get into graduate school have a vision of helping change the world for the better (academic degrees typically do not lead to the highest paying jobs, but often aim at social benefit— from clinicians in psychology and social work, to teachers, historians, and humanists, to research scientists, many graduate students are motivated by a hope of helping society). But such positive motivations can fade when the

The challenge for each adult is to take responsibility for his or her own life. What really matters to you? Does getting the dissertation really matter? This is your life: what would serve you best? That's a question to which I'll return.

This section is about trusting oneself. Time is valuable and vacillation can be painful and costly. Make a choice; trust your instinct; work on it. You can always reconsider tomorrow. But at any given moment, just try something; take some action. When problems arise—as they always do— you may have to make new plans. Trust yourself to make a good choice and to act on it, even if some previous plans have gone awry. Pragmatically speaking, it's much more effective to spend a day reading or writing something you don't use than to spend the day wondering what to do. Don't let self-doubt lead to paralysis. Trust yourself and take some action, even if the action's results are uncertain.

Ultimately, it is your project: trust yourself to do it!

CHAPTER 2:
EFFECTIVE PERSPECTIVES
ON THE DISSERTATION

Despite the horror stories that surround them, and the true difficulties they present, dissertations are not intended to make students suffer, and looking at dissertations that way doesn't provide much guidance for effective action. There are realistic perspectives on the dissertation that do provide effective guidance. These perspectives are no mystery, though they are the kind of idea that people take for granted due to familiarity. Effective action is guided by seeing and understanding what the dissertation does expect: that you express your own ideas, derived from your own research. The richer and clearer your view of the process, the more effective your efforts. Whatever the situation or difficulty, a good perspective will help guide effective action, but sometimes finding the most useful perspective requires stepping back from the project, to consider all the different angles.

GETTING THE BEST OF THE DISSERTATION

The title of this book plays on a double meaning. Often when people speak of "getting the best of something," it is in an adversarial context: one "gets the best" of an opponent or enemy. Dissertations are often seen as enemies, but they need not be seen that way. A dissertation is a big challenge, but it is the challenge of the creator, not the challenge of the combatant. Through the struggle with your work, you create. And just like the artist who sacrifices for his or her work, there is benefit to be found.

A cynical perspective says that the dissertation is nothing more than a chance to get a degree (which is not, itself, to be scorned), but that would be like suggesting that the only rewards an artist receives are the rewards of fame and money from selling a work.

John Keats famously wrote, "beauty is truth, truth beauty." I'm inclined to believe that the difference between the scholar and the artist is that the artist seeks beauty for the truth therein, while the scholar seeks truth for the beauty it contains. If you have ever been consumed with curiosity and then experienced the gratification of finding the answer, or if you have ever felt awe at the elegance of the answer to a question, or the insight of a work of scholarship, then perhaps you can understand the beauty that the scholar sees in the pursuit and discovery of truth. And, like the artist, the scholar can find a deep personal reward in the scholarly exploration. Even if you do not plan on a scholarly career, you can still find gratification in developing a deeper understanding of the field in which you intend to work. To really get the best of your dissertation— to see the beauty and interest that can be found there—it helps to see the multiple facets of the work.

Academic or professional

Whether you plan an academic career or a professional one, you can try to excel by developing a sophisticated, up-to-date understanding of the theoretical discourse in your field of endeavor. Whether architect, artist, clinician, manager, researcher, teacher, or any other career in which skill, judgment, and expertise are needed, you can choose to approach your work with the kind of curiosity that makes the search for knowledge interesting and rewarding.

NEW PERSPECTIVES AND NEW APPROACHES

Working with your dissertation over weeks, months, and even years, you will have to address several different issues:

- There is research—the search for knowledge—and all its myriad demands, like reading the work of other scholars and gathering data, not to mention doing your own thinking (and I hope that you make time for this!).

- There is writing: How do we face the blank page? How do we put our ideas down in words? Writing, as you probably have already experienced, is quite different from research, at least inasmuch as we see research and writing to be distinct. (There are ways in which writing is intertwined with research, but that is yet another concern.)

- There is also project and time management: You have a limited set of resources—your time, your effort, your money, etc.—and you have to do as much as possible with them. Chances are you're pushing the limits of those resources and still wishing you were getting better results. This book is intended to help you find ways to use your resources more effectively.

Each of these views of the work can give useful insights, and many dissertation writers—especially those who are getting stuck—can profit from re-assessing the project, using new perspectives to re-orient efforts.

Also, as you get deeper into the project, and as you face more difficulties, it is easy to lose sight of the good things in your work. It can be very helpful to remember to good aspects of the dissertation as well as the all-too-present difficulties.

The project of writing a dissertation is not just a test imposed upon you by an institution; it is an opportunity for learning and self-discovery. It is an opportunity to pursue your interests. You will face difficulties, to be sure, but what worthy endeavor is free of difficulty?

You'll certainly feel better about your dissertation work if you keep the positive aspects in mind—especially when you're in danger of feeling overwhelmed by the difficulties, and losing sight of the interests that initially moved you—and you'll probably work more productively, too. These claims are not just pie-in-the-sky optimism, but are rather based on empirical work, both in general psychology, like Mihalyi Csikszentmihalyi's work on "Flow" and "optimal experience" (1991), as well as work focused more specifically on academic writers (see, e.g., Boice, 1990).

DIFFERENT PERSPECTIVES OF THE SAME THING

It is possible to get stuck looking at a difficulty from a single perspective. In these cases it is useful to remember other perspectives—to remember to see the entire forest, not just the trees. It is for this that the artist steps back from the easel. Inasmuch as we want to use the best information possible when making plans, it is beneficial to have a full view of the dissertation's different perspectives, and to be able to choose among those perspectives to find a useful course of practical action.

If something can be viewed in multiple ways, we want to be open to all the different possibilities, not locked into just one, which can then limit our responses—both practical and emotional. The cliché of the half-full/half-empty glass is a well-known example of this general principle. The glass is, of course, both half-full and half-empty; both perspectives are true at the same time. The cliché is most familiar in comparing optimist and pessimist, and to promote focusing on the positive side. But the underlying principle—that both of the perspectives are equally true—is powerful and can be expanded beyond the scope of the simple full/empty (or good/bad) dichotomy. There's vast complexity immanent in the half-full/half-empty glass. We can ask about the contents: Water or wine? Elixir or poison? We can ask what the contents can be used for: maybe that elixir will save a life? Maybe that poison can be used to kill a rat? We can talk about uses of the glass itself—maybe we don't want a drink, but rather we want to store some fluid. We can ask about the glass itself: Is it clean? Is it nice to drink out of? Is it beautiful? Valuable? When we start to see all the different possible perspectives of a single situation, we can often find one (or more) to help guide us to a positive outcome. Like most real-world situations, there are many different aspects to the dissertation. The more aspects we see, and the richer our understanding of what is involved, the better we are able to make productive choices.

The perspectives presented in this book all provide insights concerning practical issues that dissertation writers face. Many of these perspectives try to place the dissertation into a larger context. As said earlier: we don't want to lose sight of the forest while examining specific trees. With a project like a dissertation, which takes up so much time and effort, it's easy to become focused on a specific problem, and to thereby lose sight of the larger set of ideas that motivated the work in the first place. In such situations, it is useful to step back for a moment and to look at the larger context.

MAXIMIZING VALUE

The many views presented in this book are intended to help you see value and meaning in the dissertation as a whole, and in the different tasks that you face, so that you can act more efficiently.

If you want to focus on trying to survive the battle against your dissertation, you can, even if that makes the project miserable. I know some people who believe they work best under pressure, but, speaking personally, I work better when I have time. It is important to find what is effective and efficient for you.

But even accounting for differences between personal motivational and work styles, I suggest that you'll benefit from asking how you can maximize your benefit from all the time, effort, and money that you invest. If you're thinking about surviving the dissertation, then you may feel stress or even distress. If you're thinking about how to profit from it—not only from the completed work, but from what you can learn while doing it— then, at the very least, you're taking an optimistic perspective that will help you feel better about your work, even if it does not create positive opportunities. Again, I'm not claiming that dissertations are all fun, games, and profit, but if you don't look for the potential value, you won't maximize your benefit.

To see how to get the best of your dissertation, we'll take a step back from your personal research and from any specific field of study and talk about the dissertation from a set of perspectives that can provide concrete guidance for productive engagement with your dissertation (or almost any other large, scholarly work). Central in this is to step away from the immediate goals of your specific research to look at how the dissertation is a means to achieve larger goals—for you, for your school, and for the academic community at large.

WHAT IS A DISSERTATION?

Dissertations vary widely between fields of study, as well as between methods of research. But even with the differences, there are several ways to look at a dissertation that are generally true for all (or nearly all) dissertations.

In this book, we will talk about how a dissertation is:

- A written work that you must complete: producing a written work is different from doing good research.

- A project whose aim is to complete a research project, including the terminal written work: managing a research project is different from answering research questions.

- Part of a practice of developing skill as a writer and researcher: research and writing are skills that develop with practice.[4]

- A story about how the world works (or worked in the past): research aims to explain or understand the world.

- A project driven by a research interest: research is driven by a guiding curiosity about the world.

- A project defined by a manageable research question or focus: specific research projects require a tight focus.

- Part of a larger research discourse: research is a community-based activity.

- A test of your ability: dissertations, the final hurdle to advanced degrees, are designed to test your ability—but they are not only a test.

---

4   I separate research and writing, but writing is integral to the process of research. Research is greatly facilitated by the ability to accurately express your ideas in words, because without that skill, it is very hard to get any help.

- A negotiation with your committee: managing people is an important skill that you can develop by thinking about what motivates the people with whom you work.

But, above all, a dissertation is:

- Part of your plan for how to have a better life. Ideally this would be obvious, but many people get stuck on the idea that the dissertation is an ordeal.

Each of these different perspectives can be useful at the right times and for the right purposes. There are other perspectives that are interesting or insightful, but in my experience these are the most useful ideas for writers/scholars, and I want to keep the book short.

A holistic view is important

It is useful to be able to look at the dissertation from many different angles, examining each perspective independently. By taking a simple, clear view, uncluttered by complexity, one can often see many useful things. But such fragmented, simplified views can also be problematic. If you can integrate the different views of the dissertation, they provide better guidance than working with each alone. For this reason, the book starts with, and strongly emphasizes the importance of, keeping your overall life goals in mind as the source of meaning for the other perspectives.

But the holism I refer to is not fully addressed by the overarching vision of life goals. There is also a concern that in looking at each of the individual perspectives, each becomes distorted by that focus. For example, this book separates research from writing, but writing and research are intertwined. There is an important interplay between them: The way that you write about your research will influence the way that you think about and pursue your research—it is an interplay worthy of discussion, but I will not discuss it at length. But, despite such interactions, it is still useful to talk about each perspective individually.

There are many different perspectives that can serve a writer, and separating them out from the larger project makes them easier to see, but ultimately your greatest benefit comes when you can see these different perspectives as part of a rich, integrated, and accurate picture of the dissertation project so that you can plan an effective course of action.

CHAPTER 3:
LIVING WELL

The most important perspectives to consider are those that motivate the work: Why are you doing it at all? What are the larger life goals that motivated entering a doctoral program? What purposes does the dissertation serve? How will it serve them? And what are the sacrifices you must make to achieve these ends? Has the dissertation become a battle for survival? Can you finish your dissertation without ruining your life? Plan as if the dissertation is meant to support your life; don't plan as if it requires you to sacrifice your life.

LIVING WELL IS THE BEST REVENGE

Sometimes, in response to my youthful complaints, my father would say, "living well is the best revenge." He knew the expression from F. Scott Fitzgerald (one of his favorite authors), but it is a Spanish proverb. I like it here because it works with the book's title. Like the book's title, it can be read from both a combative interpretation (when "getting the best of" means "defeating") and a creative one.

If we think about the proverb as a guide to action, what kind of action is suggested? In the adversarial reading, we can focus on the revenge—"Here's my plan to get back at them!" But looking again, I wonder whether the proverb isn't really saying: "Stop worrying about the past losses for which you seek revenge; go on and do the things you want to do." In this view, living well may not be the best revenge in terms of getting back at an enemy, but it is the best in terms of what you get from your action.

What really interests me in this book is living well. People go into graduate school with hope and optimism—if nothing else they hope to get a better job than the one they could have otherwise gotten. Too many students get stuck trying to finish work that has become drudgery. But it doesn't have to be that way.

This part of the book considers four different issues. One—the perspective of the good life—is interested in the importance of understanding what you are trying to accomplish and keeping an eye looking towards your goals—all your goals, not just the goal of finishing the dissertation. The next—the perspective of practice—emphasizes the value of practice and the relationship between practice and the development of skill. Beyond the basics of practice, there is the need to develop "momentum" in your work and practice. The final concern is to argue that sometimes the best things in life are difficult to identify and attain.

CHAPTER 3.1
LIVING A BETTER LIFE

What are your life goals? If you're like most dissertation writers, you have a larger purpose in mind; you're not just aiming to write a dissertation. Whether you plan an academic or professional career, by keeping long-term priorities in mind, you will make better decisions than you would if focused only on more immediate demands. By keeping long-term priorities in mind, you can develop a healthy relationship with your dissertation instead of letting it take over your life.

THE GOOD LIFE

We all want to live a good life, I think, but different people have different views on what constitutes a good life. Some people seek money, others fame, others moral or religious probity, others some combination of these. I will not try to help you figure out what you view as important to a good life; I will enjoin you to keep your larger goals in mind.

It is, perhaps, obvious that we want to live well. But we do not always notice that which is obvious. In particular, it can become easy to take familiar things for granted. It's good to sometimes attend to those things that you generally take for granted, because our ideas, needs, and desires change, and such changes may not be reflected in action if our behavior is governed by assumptions that we have been taking for granted.

Over the years, I have worked with some dissertation writers who didn't know what they wanted—either in life or in academia. For such a person, finding a goal—even if only finishing the dissertation—is an important first step. If you have no aim or purpose, it's hard to generate sufficient focus to finish any project.

More frequently I have worked with writers who once had clear goals, but who lost sight of those goals during their years of study and under the distress of trying to write the dissertation. For these people, the task often became immeasurably easier once they were able able to remember and focus on their earlier motivation.

There are also many who do an admirable job of keeping priorities in order, and their work is eased because of it.

Whatever may be true for you, understanding how you want to live can be important when dealing with a larger research/writing project like a dissertation. A dissertation can take over your life and have high costs. It is important to keep the costs of pursuing the project suitable to the larger context of your life.

WHY ARE YOU WRITING A DISSERTATION?

If you want to get the best of your dissertation, start with a sense of purpose!

Why are you writing a dissertation? Is the dissertation itself the goal? Or is it one step on the road to reaching some greater goal?

For most people, a dissertation is a means to an end, not an end in itself. Most immediately and obviously, a dissertation fulfills the requirements for an advanced degree. For most people, the degree itself is not the goal, but rather a qualification that allows some further aim—for example to work as a professor, to do research, to work as a clinician, or in any of the many other roles that require a doctoral degree. And the career itself is not the end either, but a means to the larger end of living well.

Whatever your aims for your life, I'll wager that you didn't enter your doctoral program thinking: "I'll sacrifice my health and financial well-being so that I can finish my dissertation, and once I've done that, I will have accomplished everything I ever wanted." When a dark day of frustration and tedium hits, it is good to have the emotional foundation provided by a sense of purpose and a sense of how the difficulties of the moment serve your larger aims.

GOALS WITHIN GOALS AND COMPETING GOALS

Goals are often complex. Actions can serve multiple different goals and different levels of goals. As noted above, the dissertation serves getting the degree, which serves getting the job, which serves having a good life. We can also see parallel goals: in addition to serving personal career goals, a dissertation might also serve some other purpose—social justice, improved medical or clinical practice, resolution of some technical problem, etc.

These goals can sometimes compete. Resolving such competing aims can be quite difficult, but it is absolutely necessary. Finding good compromises between competing ends can serve to heighten effective action. We might find, for example, that our career goal leads us to want to both apply for a job and work on our dissertation—but time limitations and deadlines might force us to choose between the two tasks. More commonly, dissertation writers find themselves choosing between their work and their social life or their work and their health. Making good decisions in such cases is aided by keeping a good perspective on your larger goals: the dissertation ought not work against your larger goals.

Understanding these nesting and competing goals may introduce difficult complexity in our decision-making process, but keeping a clear vision of the different levels of goals and the ways different goals compete can help us make effective decisions.

DO YOU REALLY WANT TO WRITE A DISSERTATION?

This is a crucial question to ask. When the going gets tough, self-doubt adds a layer of difficulty. Many dissertation writers doubt whether it's worth it, and then spend energy trying to decide whether or not to continue. If you have any doubts, it's worth thinking the question through carefully, so that you can choose whether to commit to the project and avoid the time spent wondering whether to continue.

There are really good reasons to quit a dissertation. Maybe the goals that got you in to your program have changed—maybe you want to do something else with your life than you thought you did a few years ago.

A dissertation is hard work, no matter how you slice it. There are times when it will not be enjoyable. There are times when it will be very frustrating. Even if everything goes really smoothly, there will still be real costs in terms of time and money involved in finishing your work. All of these might make it seem appealing to quit the dissertation.

If you don't want to write a dissertation, what is it that you will do? What will give your life meaning? If you are doubting, reconsider your life goals and the dissertation's place in them. And then make a plan that helps you reach your goals.

Differentiate between the small doubts that arise in the face of surmountable difficulties, and the more significant shifts in your life goals.

Don't stop working on your dissertation because you're unhappy and frustrated and then end up surfing the web. That's unlikely to make you any happier. But if you've got something real that you'd rather do—a real career, a real vocation—then pursue it! The life goals are what really matter, don't let present, temporary difficulties put you off your path.

Everyone is different, but my general feeling is that if you got into a Ph.D. program, you'll probably benefit from finishing. But not always. Make sure that you want to—that it's meaningful to you. And if so, hold to that decision when things get frustrating.

PRACTICAL CONCERNS

There are three specific practical concerns related to living a good life that I would like to mention. Setting priorities about your dissertation can impact practical decision making, and in some cases can lead to problematic patterns of behavior. (1) The dissertation itself can become the barrier between you and a good life. (2) Living well, generally, enhances your ability to work effectively. (3) Looking at the dissertation as an obstacle can be the difference between working and procrastinating.

Much of what I have to say here is obvious. But again, people often take the obvious for granted. Focusing on one issue may keep us from seeing other perspectives. We lose sight of the forest for the trees, as the saying goes. Many people I've known or worked with have lost sight of these principles when absorbed with their work. I know people who have worked themselves to ill-health while working on a dissertation they didn't care about, while deferring other things that they really wanted to do. When you focus on the goal of living well, you make different decisions than those you would make if focused solely on the dissertation itself.

Is the dissertation a barrier between you and what you want to do?
The ability of a dissertation to derail one's life should not be discounted. Academia is a "publish-or-perish" world, and that really starts with "publishing" your written work as a student: if you stop turning in written work, you will not be long for academia.

If you have already advanced to candidacy and have nothing left but your dissertation, you may be able to string out your status as a student for many, many years without writing anything more than occasional annual assessments of your progress. But is that what you want? To be a doctoral candidate until you quit or are asked to leave?

As previously mentioned, the difficulty that people associate with dissertations can be seen in the titles of long-published books like *Surviving your Dissertation* (Rudestam & Newton) or *How to Complete and Survive a Doctoral Dissertation* (Sternberg).[5] In bad cases, working on a dissertation can lead to declining emotional and physical health—hardly a desirable outcome.

The dissertation is something that should serve you. You should not be held captive to the dissertation's demands. At the least, if you measure things in terms of how they serve your goals for your life, rather than in terms of how they serve your dissertation, then you are less likely to put yourself in a situation where surviving your dissertation becomes a question.

Are you supporting your productivity by maintaining your health (both emotional and physical)?
Poor health is no fun; you obviously would rather not develop or exacerbate some medical condition as a result of your work on your dissertation, especially

---

5   Sternberg is still in publication after 30 years, which attests, at least in part, to the strength of its title. It's a good book, but the title strongly points toward a particular negative mindset.

not a condition that would then prevent your finishing the dissertation. If your work process is destroying your health, doesn't it make sense to ask whether the costs are worth the benefit you will get out of the dissertation?

Sometimes there is a benefit to be gained from sacrificing your health to work harder—if, perhaps, a deadline is imminent, then it makes sense to overwork for a few days—but in general you should remember that good health enhances your ability to work effectively. Are the short-term gains from working hard worth it if they decrease your ability to work in the future? Is the benefit of working all night worth the cost of getting less work done the next day?

One can expect to take a year writing a dissertation, if not more. It is the rare dissertation writer that finishes in less. At the least, the dissertation writer needs to be able to work consistently for many months. If physical health fails, then the ability to work, and thus the ability to complete the project in a timely fashion, is drastically reduced. And, of course, if our physical health fails, there's not only the problem of not being able to work, there's also the very real pain of the infirmity, not to mention any costs of medical treatment, and other impacts of ill health. Physical infirmity carries with it some danger of corresponding emotional difficulty.

Emotional health is important, too. When we are emotionally distressed, it is harder to work, and harder to focus. When our brains are in a state of stress and anxiety, our higher reasoning powers are inhibited by the freeze-flight-or-fight parts of our nervous system. And there is the physiological toll of poor emotional health as well: Stress can lead to difficulty sleeping and sometimes to more serious medical ramifications. Additionally, poor emotional health tends to inhibit activities that promote physical health.

For these reasons, maintaining health is important for being able to work productively for extended periods. Health allows you to finish your work sooner and health helps make things more enjoyable. While this seems rather obvious, I've known many dissertation writers who were sacrificing their health. Making your health a priority will help you finish sooner rather than later.

Does the dissertation stop you from doing things you want and need to do?
If you give up everything else in your life so that you can work on your
dissertation, you may end up hindering your work process through
resentment or resistance. If you create a situation where you resent the
dissertation for keeping you from other things, you may start procrastinating.
This is the conclusion of psychologist Neil Fiore, who once worked as a
counselor to graduate students at the University of California at Berkeley
(Fiore, 1989). Fiore observed that, generally, those students who struggled
with procrastination were those who let their work interfere with other
things in their lives, like exercise, play, or socializing. By contrast, those who
worked productively were also engaged in many different activities, so that
their lives were well-rounded, rather than dominated by the dissertation
above all else. It seems almost common sense that resentment might
contribute to procrastination. It is not hard to imagine a negative feedback
loop where dislike of the dissertation and desire to be elsewhere contribute
to working poorly, which then leads to forgoing some other fun activity,
which leads to greater dislike and desire to be elsewhere, and so on.

IN CONCLUSION

There's little doubt that a completed doctoral dissertation can lead to
better opportunities, better jobs, and a better life. There are good reasons
that people choose to pursue doctoral study, despite all the horror stories
of ABDs and jobless PhDs. But there is a real danger that the project
becomes a problem that sabotages your health or other parts of your life.
Therefore, the first and most important perspective from which to view
your dissertation is the perspective from which you view all the goals you
have set for your life. Don't let the dissertation ruin your life. Keep it in
perspective: you will work more effectively on your dissertation if the rest
of your life is healthy.

PRACTICE AND DEVELOPMENT OF SKILLS

Whatever your larger goals, you serve them by developing a regular practice that develops your skills and abilities. When you work on research, you call into action many abilities that will be refined and honed as you work. The more you practice, the better your general ability, and the better your general ability, the easier it is to deal with any task.

As I have been arguing in the previous section, your dissertation project and work should help you in achieving your most important goals. Making good plans is important for this, but as I have discussed, plans are uncertain, at best. The real foundation for a successful dissertation project is a writing and research practice that can help you improve your abilities and can help you keep moving when plans need to be revised.

SKILL AND PRACTICE

No one would argue that practice helps athletes, musicians, actors, and other performers perfect their craft. No one would argue that practice helps artists draw or paint or sculpt better. But somehow, when it comes to writing, people think that practice doesn't matter. "I can't write," or "I'm not a good writer," people tell me, as if it is fixed in stone. Your ability as a writer is not fixed. If you practice regularly, your skill will improve.

Physiological and neurophysiological change

When an athlete practices, he or she develops muscles that aid in the process. So, too, the sculptor, painter, or musician: each develops fine muscular control that allows precise manipulation of their tools. In addition, the person of skill may develop sensitivity to the details of the work: an athlete becomes sensitive to equipment; the musician develops a sensitivity to the particular instrument he or she uses. Other senses may develop through practice. The palate of a wine connoisseur makes distinctions that the tyro does not. A former cabinet-maker once said to me, "When I was building cabinets, I could see $1/32^{nd}$ of an inch accurately; now that I don't build, I can't." It is not so clear what neurophysiological change accompanies the practice of writing—there's no obvious growth of a muscle group, for example, or of some sensory acuity—but this doesn't mean that there is no neurophysiological change.

Intellectual change

The practicing athlete develops awareness of the nuances of the sport: A golfer learns a course; a tennis player learns strengths and weaknesses of opponents; players on team sports learn to run set plays and cooperate with their teammates. For the research writer, the intellectual development that comes with practice is more obvious than the neurophysiological change: when a researcher learns of new data that they can use or when they decide to approach their questions with a methodological of theoretical approach, the changes are obvious.

You, the writer, can develop your skills through practice—in both the neurophysiological aspects that support the work, as well as familiarity with the process and project. Through practice, you become a better writer, regardless of your limitations.

PRACTICE HELPS IN ALL AREAS OF ENDEAVOR

In writing the book, I initially put these ideas in the section about writing. Writing is a skill that develops through practice in a very concrete fashion: each revision of a draft helps to improve your understanding of both the material and its written presentation. On revision, however, I realized that the same considerations are true for research, though perhaps a little less obviously.

The primary value of this perspective lies in recognizing that whatever your problems as a writer or researcher today, you can improve your skills, making it easier to work and to deal with the problems you face. Just as a musician, athlete, or any skilled artisan improves through practice, so, too, does the scholar benefit.

The dissertation is probably the largest research/writing project you have ever undertaken. It may be the largest project you ever write. But if you are writing a dissertation, you are in a field where writing is a valuable skill. Writing, of course, is almost always a valuable skill, but all the more so for any person who hopes to enhance their career with a doctoral degree (or any advanced degree). Whether sending one-page e-mails, writing job applications, or applying for grants, there will be plenty of opportunities in life to use writing skills. Although the task of writing a large work is substantially different from the task of writing a small work, skill as a writer translates across contexts. Speaking generally, skill as an academic writer depends on the ability to effectively communicate ideas and to present reasonable arguments—abilities that are valuable in both speech and writing, whether as an academic or a professional.

PROFESSIONAL VS. ACADEMIC

If you are hoping for an academic career, then writing a dissertation is essentially the first of many such research/writing projects that you'll undertake, so the skill you develop writing your dissertation will serve you well through all your efforts at publication that follow. If you're looking for a professional career, chances are that you will still find plenty of opportunities to use your skills as a researcher and writer.

WRITING AND RESEARCH ARE TASKS OF GREAT COMPLEXITY AND SUBTLETY

You may be familiar with stories of authors struggling to find "le mot juste" (French for "the precise/correct/exact word"); you may well be familiar with the experience yourself. Whether you are an artist or a scholar, it can be hard to find the right word for a situation, for any number of reasons— perhaps there is no word for an idea, or no word that seems to fit quite right; perhaps the best word is one that is sometimes used in different ways, which might contribute to confusion. The problem of finding the right word arises because skilled practitioners of any art or skill are sensitive to fine distinctions.

Scholars need to make fine distinctions between points. You may be concerned with developing a set of ideas that are similar to other ideas, but with some significant distinction. Or you may be pursuing a question that others have not pursued, which requires you to refine or develop research techniques. When you are trying to understand and explain that which has not yet been explained—in short, when you are engaged in research—you are often in a context where the ideas and evidence that concern you differ in some significant way from the ideas and evidence that are commonly discussed, and thus may not have words to describe them. Languages don't always contain precise words for the things we think about, which is why words get imported from one language to another (and thus, e.g., we find the German word "schadenfreude" in English dictionaries: there was no corresponding English word, but the concept is meaningful to English speakers). We can similarly explain the existence of jargon: specialists want to talk about the fine details of their area of expertise, details which most people never talk about, and which, therefore, don't have words that refer to them. Daniel Kahneman describes this phenomenon in his own work with a comparison to the field of medicine: "To be a good diagnostician, a physician needs to acquire a large set of labels . . . Learning medicine consists in part of learning the language of medicine. A deeper understanding of judgments and choices also requires a richer vocabulary than is available in everyday language" (Kahneman, p. 3). To specialize requires uncommon understanding, and describing uncommon understanding requires uncommon language to describe accurately the subtle yet significant distinctions that are not part of common discourse.

Whether or not your research deals in concepts that have no corresponding words, you will be working in an area where fine shadings of words and concepts are significant, which makes writing difficult. Further, since your work is supposed to have some element of originality, it may well depend on talking about something that no one has talked about before, or it may look at something in a way that it has never been examined before. Both of these situations challenge conventional use of language. And so writing becomes difficult because you are trying to explain elusive, complex, and subtle ideas so that they are understood.

There is no way to eliminate these difficulties without eliminating the possibility that research will challenge our previous conceptions. As a researcher, this makes sense: research is about gaining understanding of areas where our knowledge is limited or otherwise flawed. But as a writer trying to communicate, this novelty creates difficulty. All the same, from a practical perspective, if you practice and thereby develop your abilities to recognize and express important subtle distinctions, the difficulties you face will be less severe.

DEVELOPING SKILL AS A RESEARCHER AND WRITER

Writing and research are skills that can be practiced and developed. In many ways, preparing writing is little different from preparing a speech, preparing a musical performance, or preparing an athletic feat. Indeed, if people treated writing as they might treat a speech, or as they treat a performance (whether musical or athletic), they might find writing easier. Most people preparing for a speech, a musical performance, or athletic event would expect to practice it many times, and none or few would expect to get it perfect the first time. The orator, musician, or athlete might practice a speech, exercise, technique, or event many times on the very presumption that repetition would lead to future success despite current failure.

When it comes to writing, however, people can become so dismayed that their first try isn't good enough that they give up. For whatever reason—perhaps the experience of writing "one-draft wonder" papers in high-school and college, or the influence of filling in exam blue books, or perhaps it's the intimidation of thinking about how big the work is—for whatever reason, writers seem to expect to get it right (or at least mostly right) on the first try or one of the very first tries. And when it's not, they get frustrated and may even stop working at precisely the moment in which practice could be of most help.

Perhaps writing doesn't seem as amenable to practice because it takes less time to practice a 15-minute speech (or an athletic event, or a musical performance) than it does to "practice" writing a paper of several pages. Or that spending 30 minutes completely rewriting a paragraph or page seems more arduous than spending 30 minutes practicing a speech from start to finish. Perhaps the reason people don't practice in the same way is because the written work persists: it sits there and stares back at you in a way that a practiced speech does not. If you practice a speech or musical performance or athletic feat, once you are done, the event itself is gone (except for its memory). A piece of writing, by contrast, exists after you stop writing. Whatever the reason, if you have a piece of writing that you don't like, don't berate yourself for it. Learn from it and figure out how you can do better. Instead of giving up, just try it again. Explore a different angle or different approach. And remember, too, that practice also helps you build skill. Write and rewrite. Don't worry about getting it wrong; instead cultivate the belief that after enough tries you'll get it right.

Part of the benefit of practicing goes to a specific project

Practice does not just help one master mechanics, it also allows exploration of different approaches to the performance. The most immediate short-term benefit of practicing your writing is that you can explore various ways of saying the same thing, allowing you to find the best words, just as you would seek the best words for the opening line of a speech. If you try to write an idea out many times, you will come to find more elegant expressions to serve your desires.

Fearlessly throw away the unsatisfactory old version, and tell yourself that you can write a new one that is better because you know more now than when you wrote the previous version![6] Generally, it is to be hoped, there comes a day when you like the existing draft enough, or believe in it enough, that you want to revise instead of rewriting. But when you're not happy with what you've done, you don't have to labor over it trying to make incremental changes; you might be better off writing a completely new draft and exploring a new organization and presentation of ideas. While it may seem that there is less effort involved in revising an old draft, sometimes old drafts can be tremendous time sinks, especially if they are structured around old ideas.

Part of the benefit of practicing goes to general development of skill
A longer-term benefit is that as you practice, it becomes easier to find the right words when you write.

Practicing writing is not just intellectual; it is physiological.[7] Practicing uses both brain and body. Practicing writing acts on our brains and bodies just like any other practice, helping us to become better at the task. When we practice other tasks, we know they become easier. With physical tasks, the developing ease to is related to physiological changes that are often visually apparent, but for muscle memory and intellectual development there are no such obvious indications of change. The greater ease and facility that one can develop are only revealed in the practice.

People often do not associate psychological changes with physiological changes. When reading and reciting a poem in order to memorize it, who thinks, "now I'm making my neural circuits stronger and more able to remember poems, in general"? When practicing a physical event, it is

---

6 Which is not to say that you should wantonly throw away your work. Don't let a few minor perceived problems lead you to disposing a worthwhile effort! Unfortunately, it can sometimes be hard to tell which you have.

7 Of course, since intellect is based in the body—particularly in the nervous system—all intellect is physiologically based.

easy to think that the repetition trains muscles to do something, especially if it is the same action being repeated over and over. When memorizing a poem, there is no obvious physical element to the developing skill, but, because the memorization involves repetition or the exact same thing, it is easier to think of that thing being somehow "etched in the brain".[8] But with a task like writing, where variation is almost constant, and each draft matures and changes, it is not as natural (for me, at least, and for most of the scholars with whom I've worked) to imagine that constant variation creating some corresponding physiological change. Although this does not seem intuitive to me, it does seem to stand up to logical examination. It is like the improvisational skill of a musician, poet, or actor: improvisation is itself a skill that can be practiced, and writing involves the same kind of open variation.

If you already think about how practice changes your brain, then this argument about the importance of practice should make sense to you. If you don't think this way, remember: practice leads to physiological change, including change in our brains.

Practice helps you focus on the important matters—on the ideas you want to understand/communicate—rather than on the practical concerns of trying to get your tools to do what you want

As I have already said, writing is about communicating ideas, and it's hard to capture our ideas in words. It can be even harder if our attention is distracted by things other than the elusive ideas we want to express, in particular the technical and practical aspects of writing. In order to accomplish our central task of capturing ideas in words, we use various tools. These tools can distract us from the main task. To write, we use a computer, or pen and paper, or, perhaps, a voice recorder combined with

---

8   Admittedly, we do think of memory, in particular, in terms of physical changes in the brain. It is not unusual to think of rote repetition and memorization as "engraving" or "etching" something on the brain—as if the brain were a tablet on which we write—or as "storing something"—as if the brain were a container, which is a metaphor that the fictional character Sherlock Holmes used to describe his memory. But those metaphors do not (to me, at least) suggest a positive growth of skill or ability, only a recording of a specific item in the brain. But memorizing one poem will help develop a general memorization skill.

dictation. These tools are very good for recording words, but sometimes they can present difficulties of their own—I daresay that anyone who has ever had trouble with their computer or word processing software knows what I'm talking about. Another "tool" that we need as writers is punctuation. We do not need punctuation when we think or when we speak, but when we put the words on the page we need punctuation because punctuation helps readers understand us. Punctuation issues can draw one's attention away from main ideas almost as effectively as word processing problems.

Every writer has a different level of familiarity and comfort with the tools and technical aspects of writing. If you find yourself struggling with word processing software or with punctuation, or with any aspect of the writing process, remember that practice will make these things easier.

If we are struggling with our tools or equipment, our attention is divided between the task and the tools, which makes the main task harder. By analogy consider driving a car or riding a bicycle: When we first learn to drive or ride, we spend considerable attention keeping the car on the road and keeping the bicycle upright. A large part of our attention is focused on operating the vehicle without crashing. But as we practice, manipulation of the vehicle becomes easier and more natural and requires less conscious attention. With sufficient experience and the consequent skill, we don't need to focus on trying to keep from crashing, and we can focus on getting to our goal. Sometimes we even have time to enjoy the view.

When you write, are you focused on your ideas? How much of your attention is on technical issues like punctuation or management of the computer software? Practice helps you get your attention off the technical issues and on to the ideas. If you are getting stuck because you're worried about spelling something wrong, or punctuating wrong . . . don't worry! Get the idea down in whatever form. Practice putting your ideas into words. There is almost always time later to go back and proofread and fix the errors of punctuation. But if the ideas aren't there . . . well, it's like driving a car without a destination.

In all these dimensions, practice can help us increase our skill and increase the facility with which we accomplish all our research and writing tasks. Research and writing will always be challenging, but as the skill develops, the nature of the challenge changes. When we start, it takes great effort to do something simple. As skill grows, the smaller problems fall away and we are faced with problems of greater complexity, richness, and interest. In short, this perspective reminds us that we will get better at our tasks if we practice, which offers the promise that the dissertation project will become easier and more interesting if we practice.

To get the best of your dissertation, develop a practice that will maintain your productivity and your efficiency. What steps can you take to improve your efficiency and productivity moving forward?

In building your practice, ask yourself:

1. What can I do to be most productive?
2. Are my patterns helping maintain productivity?

REGULAR PRACTICE
AND MOMENTUM

One of the easiest ways to make any task easier is to practice regularly and build momentum in your practice. By working regularly—every day or almost every day—you build rhythms that support work, and you don't have to spend time "getting back up to speed" on a project you haven't seen for a week. It's not easy to build up momentum on a project, but the overall effort expended is reduced if you gather momentum and keep moving.

If there is one point on which almost all books on writing (whether academic or not) agree, it is the value of writing every day (or almost every day). I have already discussed practice and the development of skill and how practice is the basis on which skills are built. But in terms of realizing a large project like a dissertation, it is not enough to have well-developed skills, the skills must be put into use.

In the first chapter, I say that if I only had one piece of advice for you, it would be to trust yourself. If I were to give only one additional piece of advice, it would be to work on your project every day, or as close to every day as possible, even if only for fifteen minutes.[9]

KEEP IDEAS FRESH BY PRACTICING

Finishing a dissertation requires effective management of a large, complex project. In addition to the myriad theoretical and scholarly concerns related to developing coherent and original research, there are the numerous practical concerns related to the project, ranging from acquiring needed materials and finding time to do the work to keeping track of the many

---

9   One of my favorite dissertation writing books is the popular *Writing Your Dissertation in Fifteen Minutes a Day* by Joan Bolker.

deadlines and commitments. This complexity cannot be eliminated. By working on the project regularly, you can keep more of the project fresh in your mind. There are two kinds of freshness that arise from regular practice.

The first of these is the freshness of familiarity—the ability to keep many complex ideas in mind. Imagine a professional musician who needs to play a long, complex piece of music. When the musician plays or practices the piece regularly, all the details remain fresh and in order, and the piece can be played without hesitation and without sheet music. If that same musician puts the piece aside for a month or a year, even if the musician's general skill increases, they might need to review and practice the work before playing it, just to make sure that all the pieces are in order and the needed pieces will be present during the performance. Similarly, the dissertation writer who works every day keeps much closer contact with the complexities of the work—seeing plans for development, problems with the current task, and so forth—and can act in accordance with those complexities. In particular, if you worked on the project recently, there is a good chance that as you ended your last work session, you had ideas about where to go when you next worked. If the work is put aside for a week or more, or even for several days, ideas that were fresh fade. The idea that you didn't have time to develop fully in your last work session—an idea that seemed so clear at the moment you were working—will not necessarily seem so clear if you try to recover it after a delay.

The other kind of freshness is the freshness of novelty. Novelty arises for two reasons. The first reason that novelty arises from a regular practice is simply that we make more progress: each task is completed in fewer days. If we finish a task in five days instead of nine, that task spends less time weighing on us. Novelty also arises simply because we are more engaged in the project: if we practice regularly, we have the task on our minds more, even when we're not working. This extra time thinking about the task can lead to new perspectives that won't arise if you're letting the idea slip out of mind and then spending effort just to get back to the idea you had previously. I will note, however, that novelty does often have costs: in particular, new ideas often call for revision of previous work, and that can cause delays.

WRAP IT UP BEFORE IT CHANGES

We learn as we live. The more time that elapses while engaged in a project, the more time there is for your ideas to change, or for something to come up that calls for a change in your plan of action. The most extreme example of this would be if someone published work similar to what you were trying to accomplish. Such a publication could force significant changes in your work, and though such changes might benefit the research, they are almost certain to delay it.

Obviously, we want to embrace insights that help us, and it's good to have novel insights that challenge our way of thinking. But, speaking pragmatically, wouldn't it be better to finish the dissertation, get the degree, and then use the new insight to start a new research project as a Ph.D.?

By keeping your momentum going, and by keeping the project fresh, you are more likely to be able to keep up progress without major changes. And then you can finish one project and move on to a new one.

DO SOMETHING EVERY DAY

More than anything else (other than trusting yourself!), I recommend making a regular practice, an everyday practice, if possible. Do something every day. Get in the habit of working on the project. Get in the habit of thinking about the project. Every time you work on the project you make it fresher in your mind, and more likely to be a subject of thought in idle moments—like waiting at traffic lights, doing laundry, etc.

The more often you work on the project, the fresher it will be in your mind, and this will support more effective use of your time. When the project is fresh, you can dive right in to some new task. When you've been away from the project for a time, it's often necessary to spend some time just trying to figure out what to work on next.

Admittedly, working every day doesn't prevent you from coming to some impasse where you don't know what to do. But the more often you work, the more likely it is that you will have some idea of how to work productively than if you have set the project aside and you have to spend time just trying to re-orient yourself to the project.

You have the choice of how to spend your time. If you have decided that it is important to finish your dissertation, isn't it then worth trying to make time every day so that you can finish sooner?

INTERRUPTIONS

The world around us goes on, even if there's a dissertation to be written. The lives of our family and friends go on regardless, and many events in life call our attention away from the dissertation. Circumstances of significance—births or deaths, marriages and divorces, etc.—may well call us from our work.

When faced with such circumstances, there is still the need and opportunity to keep working on your dissertation. It is particularly in such situations that a habit of writing and working on your dissertation will be most useful in helping you move towards your goal.

Obviously there may be some events that absolutely demand every possible minute of your time, or where it is just inappropriate to turn your attention to your work. But for most of the interruptions in our lives, there is space to step back and take a little time for ourselves. In such situations, being able to grab ten or fifteen minutes to work on an idea, or even just to make a few notes regarding ideas or plans, can help keep the project fresh in your mind. You may not be able to step away from a weeping relative at a funeral, but if you try, you can grab 15 or 30 minutes to yourself if you're visiting family on a holiday.

If you feel guilty about taking time for your dissertation, just keep in mind your larger goals. And remember, too, that those larger goals affect those around you: your family may be disgruntled if you excuse yourself from some event because you're working on your dissertation, but they may also be disgruntled if your dissertation stretches on to eternity, and they will be immensely pleased when you do finish; they may even be immensely pleased just to have you make any progress.

The better you are at finding little pieces of time despite interfering circumstances, the easier it is to maintain progress towards completion. Minimizing the time lost to interruptions is extremely valuable.

TAKE THE NEXT STEP

Wherever you are in your process, it is important to keep up progress by taking a next step. Sometimes we're uncertain of what that next step should be, but we can always take some step, so that we keep the work fresh in our minds, and so that we make some progress—even if only the progress of being able to say that the last taken step was a mistake.

A book on business management expresses this idea well: "[There is] a mindset and a method of attacking problems . . . The mindset is that you don't have to create a big block of time or an extensive campaign to get something useful started. Some useful work can be done today, *no matter how little time is assigned*. That piece of work will suggest another useful action—yours or someone else's—and doing this consistently will lead to real progress." (Wright, 1990, p.15, emphasis added).

The value of this approach is at least partly based on the idea that "No *single* thing can be done to succeed — it takes a thousand small things *all* done well" (Wright, 1990, p.16, emphasis in the original).

In carrying out the entire project that is a dissertation, there are many, many things to be done, and many things to learn on the way. And sometimes there will be mistakes. If you persist in taking small steps, one after another, you will still make progress, even when some of the steps go wrong. Things that go wrong often provide valuable information about your project, so even a mis-step can help give you better guidance for the future.

Focusing on small steps can also help with your emotional state. With large projects that stretch over a long period of time, there are many different issues that need to be addressed; this multiplicity of concerns can be confusing, distracting, and ultimately distressing. By keeping an eye on a next step—some action of some sort—you remain focused on something that you can handle, even when the scope of the overall project seems overwhelming. If you focus on a small next step—any action that moves you forward just a little—a reference that you needed to find, a paragraph that you wanted to revise, a single source that you wanted to read, even making a to-do list—you can put aside the stress of managing many things at once and make a little progress on something small but necessary. And making progress will support your emotional state.

THE DOWNWARD SPIRAL AND THE UPWARD SPIRAL

The projects upon which we work have emotional impact: when things go well, we feel good; when things go poorly, we feel bad. In working on an extended project, this emotional dynamic can be crucial, especially with respect to self-reinforcing patterns of feedback.

It's pretty easy to get stuck in a downward emotional spiral. If something goes wrong and we miss a goal, then we feel bad. And, feeling bad, it can be hard to get started on work, which impedes progress. Each day that passes without making good progress contributes to the sense that we are stuck and to doubts as to whether have what it takes to finish. Further, each day that we don't make progress is another day that we return to the same ideas—and so instead of facing fresh ideas and fresh problems, we keep coming back to the same thing, which contributes to a sense of drudgery and frustration. And with each passing day of frustration, the emotional distress and sense of difficulty can increase.

On the other hand, it's possible to initiate an upward spiral. If we get a piece of work done, we often feel good at having made progress, and this progress boosts our confidence to take the next step, which makes that next step easier, thus boosting our progress further, thereby reinforcing our confidence. The more momentum we have on an upward spiral, the easier it is to keep moving past some non-research interruption, or past some research-related difficulty. And, the more progress we make, the more we are working with fresh ideas. If we have been making progress and feeling good about it, and if our interest is high because we are engaged with fresh ideas, then we are more likely to want to get back to work after being interrupted. And if we've been working regularly and making progress, when we discover some error in our previous work, it feels less important, because of our general experience of making progress.

It's easy to get into the downward spiral—after all, it doesn't take much energy to do no work. There are, however, costs to not making progress. The most immediate cost is the emotional burden of not making progress. But in the long run, financial costs and interpersonal costs also become significant. Financially there are fees to paid, as well as loss of potential income. Interpersonally, lack of progress can strain relationships with professors, colleagues, family, and friends. The downward spiral is easy to start, but the long term costs are high. The upward spiral is harder to start and keep going. It requires constant effort to keep making progress. But progress has its rewards, so although the upward spiral has a high cost of entry, the return on the investment is high enough that the benefits outweigh the costs.

IF YOU'RE STUCK, WRITE ABOUT IT

If you're ever wondering what to do next, and this uncertainty is keeping you from making progress, write about it. Write down what you're thinking about. Write down the problems you face. Write down things that you could do. Write about what you do want to do, and why. Write about what you don't want to do, and why. If you're having conceptual difficulties in your work, practice writing them down.

Some of the questions you could address:

- What are you stuck on?

- What is the main issue?

- What is one specific problem you're faced with?

- What are possible approaches to that problem?

These questions can be applied in almost any situation. Can't decide which book or article to read? Write about the works that you're considering—

what's good about them? What's bad? What parts of it agree with the work you've already done? If you do this, you'll have a written record of the book that you may be able to use later, but more importantly it will help you focus your attention on possible next steps with respect to that work.

When you're stuck, writing about your "stuckness" is a warmup practice: it helps you find ideas and get moving without any of the pressure to get things right. The point is not to create something that you share with others, so don't worry about its quality or what others would think of it. Use it to tease out different possibilities and find useful steps that could move your dissertation forward. Such writing has the added benefit of practicing writing and helping you develop your writing skill.

CHAPTER 3.4
THE BEST THINGS IN LIFE

The dissertation can be a positive experience, but even if everything goes exactly according to plan, there's a lot of work required, as well as a significant commitment of time and money. What are you going to get from the dissertation? And what are the costs will you pay to get those things? If you see all the opportunities for benefit, and you can plan effectively to minimize costs, you are likely to get the best your dissertation has to offer.

As I say earlier, you are the one who must decide what a good life is for you. But no matter how you define it, I argue that the best things in that life are not free. The best things in life may not have a price tag on them, and you may not have to pay with money, but all the same, the best things in life are not free.

IS IT WORTH IT?

Writing a dissertation is far from easy, and there will likely be times when it is unpleasant. Hard work will be involved. Time and money. Frustrations. Not to mention all the things you could have done otherwise.

In economics, there is a concept called "opportunity cost," which is typically measured as the difference between the actual return on an investment and the return that the investment could have earned if put into a bank at a fixed interest rate. Basically, if I choose to buy stock in a company, then I can't put the money into an interest-bearing account whose return is guaranteed. This concept highlights how we can measure the value of an investment in terms of forgone opportunities.

Opportunity cost is relevant to all aspects of life, not just investments. Whenever we choose among options, we forgo something in favor of something else. Instead of working on a dissertation, you could be doing something else.

So, given all the costs—the work, the time, the money, the opportunity—is it worth it? Are you willing to pay the costs to get the dissertation? Is the dissertation really worth it to you? Will getting a dissertation help you lead a good life?

This book argues that there is a lot of good that can be gotten from a dissertation. There are benefits beyond just receiving a degree, and receiving a degree is no trivial benefit. The better your understanding of the process, the better your chances of both reducing costs (or avoiding unnecessary costs) and gaining benefits along the way.

THE BEST MOMENTS IN OUR LIVES

As I previously mentioned, psychologist Mihalyi Csikszentmihalyi argues that the best moments in our lives—the experiences we value most—"usually occur when a person's body or mind is stretched to its limits in a voluntary effort to accomplish something difficult and worthwhile" (Csikszentmihalyi, p.3). What we most value are those moments of challenge in which we operate successfully.[10] At first glance, it might seem that a leisure activity, like watching TV, is really fun and enjoyable, but Csikszentmihalyi argues that our appreciation and enjoyment of such easy experiences ultimately pales in comparison to the rewards from much more difficult activities.

Csikszentmihalyi argues that the best moments come when we are engaged in activities that lead to the "flow" experience, and among those activities that he explicitly lists as flow activities are both reading and writing—which, of course, are central to the work of the scholar.

There is a reason that the word "philosophy" takes a root from a word for love. There is a reason that people pursue academic careers despite the possibility of earning higher pay elsewhere. And the fact that academics

---

10   This conclusion aligns with the ideas of Frankl, mentioned earlier, in the sense that something "worthwhile," in Csikszentmihalyi's words, is likely to be "meaningful." This conclusion also agrees with literature that suggests that people find learning to be a rewarding a positive experience (e.g., Abraham Maslow's *Toward a Psychology of Being*, originally published in 1962).

theoretically get to take summers off is only a small one of those reasons.[11]

The tasks of scholarship—reading, writing, the search for evidence and understanding—are flow activities; they are challenging and they are fulfilling because of that challenge.

If you are planning a career where a doctoral degree is needed—whether professional or academic—then you are entering a field where there are challenges to your knowledge and understanding—challenges that are the basis for flow experiences. Whether a professor doing research, a clinician trying to form a treatment plan, or a public official trying to craft policy, the tasks of the researcher are are involved.

In this light, the very practice of writing a dissertation is valuable in itself, and it provides a foundation for future positive career experiences.

IT'S DIFFICULT TO RECOGNIZE THE "RIGHT THING"

In life and in research, logical certainty is elusive, but we still need to act. Making lists of pros and cons or of costs and benefits can provide a lot of useful insight, but such lists are uncertain. In the end, one must make the best decision one can based on the information one has.[12] Ultimately, as I have said before, you must trust yourself to make a decision and to act on it. It is my hope that this book will help you understand your dissertation project in a way that you can make better, more successful decisions with respect to it.

---

11   Actually, I can't recall meeting a professor who actually took summers off—a vacation, sure, but the professors I've known pretty much all worked constantly.

12   See Jean-Pierre Protzen, "Reflections on the Fable of the Caliph, the Philosopher and the Ten Architects." *Journal of Architectural Education*, 3(4): 2–8. 1981.

CHAPTER 4:

PROJECT

Shifting our view from your life as a whole in which the dissertation is part, to looking at the dissertation as a task to be carried out, we first consider the dissertation as a large project that you have to manage and bring to completion. From this perspective we can apply insights about conditions faced by those managing similar projects.

A PROJECT TO BE COMPLETED

Completing a dissertation involves many things—reading, writing, and more—and takes a long time. Managing such a project, which lasts for months or years, is not something that many dissertation writers have done. This is, I believe, part of the reasoning behind dissertations: they are meant to push students to do something new that will provide important experience that will support a career in which highly specialized knowledge is needed.

If you manage the project well, your efforts will be most efficiently directed.

WHAT COUNTS AS COMPLETION?

In order to complete a project, we need to know what counts as completion. Unfortunately, knowing when one is done may not be clear—at least from certain perspectives.

Sometimes it is obvious when something is complete. If you're doing a crossword puzzle, there's no question about whether you've answered all the clues; if you're playing chess, there's no question whether checkmate has occurred. For other things, the question of completion is more elusive. It has been said that art is never completed, only abandoned (attributed in various forms to Leonardo da Vinci and Paul Valéry). It has been said about design that there is no rule when to stop—that you stop designing only because you run out of patience, time, or money.[13] Research shares this uncertain nature: even the best research has limitations, leaving unanswered questions. If you judge the completeness of research in terms of whether you have resolved all unanswered questions, you will run out of time, patience, or money before you reach "completion."

For dissertations, there is, however, one very clear test of completion: if a dissertation is accepted by the relevant people, then it is complete. From this perspective, the nature of the project is secondary; what matters is what certain people think of the project. If you can get the right people to sign the right paperwork, your dissertation is done, regardless of what you learned or wrote. With the right signatures, a crayon scrawl could be a dissertation.[14] This perspective points out that there is a clear sign of completion for a dissertation, but it's a sign that comes from other people, not from some abstract criteria by which you judge the work. This suggests the importance of convincing your committee of your worth, which includes being able to write in a way that reaches your audience.

Although there is no definitive set of criteria to define the complete dissertation, abstract criteria are a useful guide. It can be useful to try to define some standard of completion by comparing your work to other works of the same sort, in particular, other dissertations in your program. You can recognize various dimensions that help you identify completion: length of the work, scope of question asked, completion of proposed data gathering scheme, completion of proposed data analysis scheme, completion of planned elements of the dissertation, etc. While any of these dimensions might be fungible in some way—you might decide to consider more data, or to pursue some additional analysis, or other alteration—together they combine to give an idea of what could be

---

13   This idea is from the work of Horst Rittel. See, for example, Rittel's "On the Planning Crisis" in Protzen & Harris, *The Universe of Design* (pp. 151-165).

14   I do not say this to impugn the quality of work necessary in degree-granting programs, only to point out how a work that is *prima facie* insufficient by "normal" academic standards could be considered complete from the administrative/institutional perspective.

considered a completed dissertation. If you define goals for these different criteria, you give yourself both a goal to focus action, and a sense of where to stop that doesn't require submitting a draft to anyone else—and having such an outside standard of comparison can be very useful for those of you who find yourself caught by perfectionism or constantly saying "but wait, it's not quite ready . . ." Or it can be if you choose an appropriate work for comparison—don't compare your dissertation to the magnum opus of your favorite author!

Ultimately, although you shape your work with the research-related criteria, it is the signatures that say when you are done. Therefore, while it is important to trust your own judgment, the only hard criteria you have for recognizing completion is your committee's willingness to sign, and so your journey will be facilitated by giving drafts to your committee, and learning where they set the bar for quality. Once you understand how to satisfy them, you can finish your dissertation, and get the degree.

PROJECT TIMELINES

The basic timeline of any event is simple: there is a beginning, middle, and end. Your dissertation will go through these basic stages: there will be a beginning, when the project is new to you; there will be a middle, during which the project may feel rather stale; and there will be an end, when completion seems imminent. This is a natural progression, but due to the nature of research and learning it will be unpredictable. Defining a good question can be especially difficult during research because as we learn, we develop more sophisticated understandings that can shift the question that we wanted to ask. But this basic temporal structure doesn't always translate well into a series of steps that a writer can follow.

Many books on dissertations define a specific sequence of tasks for a dissertation writer to follow. These sequences follow common models of design or problem-solving processes, in which there are some basic set of steps like: define the question; gather data; formulate a solution; check the solution.[15] This basic model would be great for dissertations, if only scholars didn't learn things that led them to need to redefine their questions or redefine their methods. If you can define a question that leads to a simple project that you can finish quickly, that's ideal. If you don't, you're not alone: defining questions is difficult. It is often that case that defining the problem is the problem.[16] For purposes of giving a recommendation to writers, my suggestion is to attempt to follow such a set of steps, but to recognize how improvisation is needed to negotiate such a process.

There is no clear demarcation between the beginning, middle, and end. To some extent, the shift from one phase to the next is determined by your attitude toward the work, and your willingness to remain committed to a single formulation of the project, not to mention the corresponding support from your faculty committee. The opportunity to redefine your question is always available, but when you redefine the question, you redefine the work needed to reach completion. Sometimes such a redefinition can lead to a quicker completion, but sometimes redefinition leads to a great deal of extra work.

Beginning

You begin when you decide to carry out a project. At the beginning, ideas are fresh and volatile, and you are exploring the scope and nature of the topic of study and setting goals for your future work. In this phase, as with the middle phase that follows, the imaginative exploration of ideas is the primary issue. To support your imaginative processes, it is important to work regularly—every day if possible—but it is also important not to overwork. Overwork and stress-creating behaviors interfere with using your imagination, and the

---

15　Models of design and problem-solving processes are often structured around a series of design phases (e.g., in the work of J.C. Jones or Herbert Simon). Many dissertation books also talk about such phases as clear-cut steps. Unfortunately, due the myriad uncertainties that most large projects face, these simple phases of design prove to be a poor reflection of the process faced by a designer or a researcher, and can therefore sometimes be a poor guide to action (see Rittel's "On the Planning Crisis" in Protzen & Harris, *The Universe of Design*, pp. 151-165).

16　Again, see Rittel's "On the Planning Crisis" in Protzen & Harris, *The Universe of Design* (pp. 151-165).

emotional component is also important: with a long road ahead, it is crucial to maintain a good relationship with your project. You don't want to start resenting your project before you've even gotten deep into it.

Practice writing at the project's beginning

The beginning is a period of exploration. Early on, it is useful to write to help focus and clarify your own ideas. Explore and experiment. Write short pieces and then rewrite them. Try to put your ideas into a formal order, but don't worry about getting things exactly right—the exercise and experimentation of formulating and reformulating the issues will help refine your ideas. Keep trying to describe the points that you feel most important.

At the beginning of the project, you don't yet know precisely what you're doing—or at least you cannot know with certainty what the final form of your work will be.[17]

The writing in the initial phase of the project should be viewed as a tool to help you develop your ideas. It is also a means to improve your writing skill as you go.

Write with the aim to define the smallest workable project that you can—smallest because projects, especially in their incipient stages, have a penchant for growing, and you want to define a project that you can complete!

At the beginning, your written pieces should be small—sentences, paragraphs, or a few pages. Such pieces should be produced quickly, with the focus on sharing your ideas with your committee and others.

Middle

When you feel that you have found a question on which to focus, and you start to develop a clear research agenda to which you will commit, you begin the middle phase. To some extent, you enter the middle phase of the project when you first generate a complete dissertation proposal. But

---

17   If you knew what your work would show before you did it, then it wouldn't be research, would it? On a certain level it should be unnecessary to say this. But I have worked with many writers who got stuck because they felt they didn't know enough. If you're engaged in research, you have to proceed in the face of uncertainty.

generating a proposal is no guarantee that things won't still change. It is, at best, a sign that you have remained committed to a single idea for an extended period.

In the middle, you are refining ideas—there is still room for exploration, but generally you have a strong enough sense of the project that you resolve problems within the framework of your question rather than redefining the question entirely.

In the middle of a project you may end up reformulating the guiding question completely because of new ideas generated as you start to deal with gathering and analyzing data, but you are still pursuing the same initial motivation that began the work, and the same general trend of inquiry.

The middle of the project is characterized by shifting ideas and developing understanding, but still with a commitment to keeping the same basic project. The middle phase can often feel like the beginning— especially if you find it necessary to redefine the question on which you work. Redefining your purpose and direction is a necessary part of the development of most projects—especially those that are dealing with territory that is new to you. But the middle phase also includes gathering the data—to some extent this is the phase in which the actual research is done. The middle phase ends about when you stop gathering data and move towards creating a final draft.

Writing during the project's middle

The middle of the project is, like the beginning, a period of exploration, though with more focus on finding answers to your questions than on finding a good question. In this period you are moving toward creating the form that will become basis of the final draft. It is the period in which you try to formulate your overall story—from your choice of focus to the conclusions that you will draw. In a way, the purpose of the middle period is to advance the draft to the point where you can get your dissertation chair or your dissertation committee to say that you've got a draft that needs revision (and maybe some rewriting), but not more research.

End

At the end of the process, you are no longer exploring, but rather are putting the project into a final written form. At this point, you are trying to wrap things up given the current definition of the project. Typically, this phase may take the least time: once you have a clear vision of where you're going, getting to the end is much easier. Although there is a lot of work that needs to be done to bring a project to completion—editing, proofreading, checking references, etc.—you have a better idea of where to go because you're reporting on completed research, and so you work faster because there are fewer choices that could reshape the work as a whole.

For the beginning and middle, I discourage working long hours on your dissertation—it's important to keep your life in balance—don't forsake your health, family, or social life. But nearing the end—when most of the work is editorial and less demanding of imagination—it often makes sense to log longer hours, especially to meet an approaching deadline. Trying to force early drafts by sitting endless hours staring at blank pages is not a winning strategy, but if you have already completed a first draft, and you have clear guidance about what to do, and you have a chance to get the dissertation done before you have to pay another term's registration fees, then the long hours are worth it (at least as long as you're being productive during the long hours and not somehow seriously injuring yourself).

Writing as you approach the project's end

The final phase of the writing project focuses on completing the one draft that you have. Early in the process, you try to resolve problems by shifting focus or reformulating your question or rewriting entire sections; at the end, you resolve problems by acknowledging them, using them to set boundaries on your work. It is not an attempt to make the work perfect by eliminating its problems, but rather an attempt to bring the work to completion despite the problems. In many fields it is expected that problems are presented in a "Limitations" section, in which are described the problems with your research that you're not going to resolve. But research is always limited: the reason that "limitations" sections are conventional is because all research has limitations. The key move for the researcher is to recognize that the standards of the research community accept this: if you have problems, and you tell your audience what those problems are, the problems are no longer a bar to making a contribution to the research community, rather the problems become a guide to help other scholars understand the implications of your work and to help others develop research that cooperates with your own.

A SERIES OF WRITING PROJECTS

A dissertation project calls for writing and rewriting. Along the way, there are various milestones that punctuate the journey. These may vary according to your institution, your field of study, and method of study. The two most basic milestones are the proposal and the final draft. Other milestones that may appear in different places in different programs are: first completed chapter draft (and any subsequent completed chapter), completed data gathering, IRB approval. Along with these milestones, there may be additional writing projects that are related to your dissertation, but are not directly tied in to any of the milestones, for example, grant and fellowship applications, conference submissions, or departmental progress reports.

Each of these written pieces can be viewed as a project in itself—each with its own beginning, middle, and end, and with its own difficulties. For many of these, the starting point will be a previous draft (for example, when trying to create the final draft of the dissertation, you will be relying on previous chapter drafts, or on the dissertation proposal). For other projects, you will necessarily start with a blank page, as you try to present your project with respect to the specific context—fellowship applications, for example, may need to include material specific to the interests of the organization granting the fellowship—and may need to be tailored to respond to specific concerns relevant to the context.

In each case—for each new submission—you are faced with the production of a work that you submit to someone else for their judgment.

In each case, there is a need to produce a final draft, which means producing preliminary drafts as well. This need to write and rewrite requires work, but while you can often re-use material from one piece to the next, writing and rewriting from scratch are often much more effective and efficient ways to proceed than trying to revise a problematic old draft. In the long run, this effort is not wasted: by writing and rewriting, you develop your skill as a writer, making each new project a little easier. And by writing and rewriting—by focusing on expressing the ideas in your head, rather than revising an old draft—you can help clarify your focal issues. Ideas are at the heart of a paper—if you can get the ideas into a good workable order, it becomes much easier to write. If old drafts have had trouble with focus, rewrite from a blank page, and once your focus is improved it becomes much easier to find material that can be reused without losing focus.

HOW LONG DOES IT TAKE?

Research projects are uncertain. We don't know exactly what they will be when we start (if we did, it wouldn't be research), and so planning a specific timeline is terribly difficult.

If everything falls into place, I think it is absolutely reasonable to believe that you can finish a dissertation in a year, or even a little less. That is if *everything* falls into place. If the first attempt at defining a problem yields a good result; if your faculty committee always responds in a timely fashion, and always approves the work with no more required revisions than can be done in the time planned for revisions; if the IRB approves your work (if necessary); if there are no serious problems getting access to the appropriate data; if there are no problem with analysis. Most of all, finishing that quickly depends on being able to remain confident and committed to your research question, so that you're not forced to redefine the whole project. If everything falls into place, then one school year is absolutely enough time to complete the project. Practically speaking, this is probably the lower boundary for the time necessary for a dissertation.

There may be no upper boundary for finishing, given that many never finish, and many work for decades or more. I once had a consultation with a man who had started his dissertation in the 1970s and had maintained his status as a doctoral candidate for over 30 years, though that is surely an extreme outlier. Data show that about 55% of students have completed within 10 years (across all fields). If we assume two to four years of course work, then those finishing in a decade worked on their dissertation for six to eight years. Eight years is a long time to work on one project. There are many projects worth working on for eight or more years, but I would suggest saving them for after you get your degree. Or, less flippantly, if you've got such a project, define some small, preliminary part of it to be your dissertation, and then finish the project once you're a doctor.

In terms of making a plan for completion, I would suggest a two-year plan: if you are able to work on a dissertation regularly with productive patterns, then, barring major problems, two years should be an eminently reasonable time to completion, and if most things work out along the way, less is possible. But in saying this, I want to emphasize that any number of problems over which a scholar has no control may intervene: taking longer than you planned is not a sign of personal failure or weakness; there are too many factors that one simply cannot anticipate at the beginning of a project.

DIFFERENT KINDS OF RESEARCH
HAVE DIFFERENT TIMELINES

Obviously, the nature of your research will directly impact the timeline and how things are done. The comments I make here will be very general; I cannot hope to cover every kind of dissertation in detail.

For those in the laboratory sciences, given the general structure of university research laboratories, the structure of your research project will, to some extent, follow the structure of other research done in your laboratory. You can get an idea of project timelines by looking at the project timelines of others in your lab.

For those in humanities, there is the least structure. Historians, philosophers, students of literature, and others will have very little limit on the nature of their research, and often engage in very open-ended projects. For a scholar whose work is derived from examination of some archive, for example, there is little way to predict what you will find, and thus it is hard to predict where the project will go. Similarly, a scholar choosing to analyze some corpus of data (e.g., the work of a specific author, or works from a specific period) may find reasons to alter the definition of the corpus. For these reasons, research projects like this entail a great danger of constantly expanding and shifting. It is much easier to limit a project that is based on a specific empirical study.

For a scholar in the social sciences doing a quantitative empirical study, the project proposal is necessarily detailed and describes the data to be gathered and the forms of analysis used. In such a study, it is difficult to come up with a plan, but once the plan has been set and approved by the committee and the school IRB (when necessary), the project is largely set, and regardless of whether the quantitative results are positive or not, the project is complete once the results have been gathered, analyzed, and reported.

Scholars doing qualitative empirical studies have less structure than those doing quantitative studies—qualitative work does not require as much preliminary definition, and, indeed, with some methods, like Grounded Theory, the course of research is highly dependent on being able to learn as you go, without harboring preconceptions. (This actually makes pure Grounded Theory a poor choice for dissertations, unless limits on the data collection plan are framed very carefully.) For many kinds of qualitative research, it is necessary to define the scope of data to be gathered and analyzed, and such definitions help limit the scope of the project: once you've done the data gathering, you can probably write up a complete dissertation, even if the results are poor or hard to interpret.

SUMMARY

The dissertation is a big project, and to get it done, and to get the best from your efforts, it's important to recognize the project-management aspects of the work. The better you understand the nature of the task before you, the better you can plan your efforts. In particular, by taking the perspective of a project manager, you focus on important aspects of the project that are separate from the questions of research and writing that are the most obvious foci for the dissertation writer. And by recognizing the uncertain nature of research projects, one can make a plan that gives good guidance for productive action, while retaining sufficient flexibility to manage unexpected developments.

CHAPTER 5:
RESEARCH

The next perspective of interest looks at research. There are a number of perspectives from philosophy of science and epistemology that provide guidance for practical action in research. There is a gap between the idealized search for truth and the practical issues of research, and often it takes some re-imagining of the nature and process of research to move from being a student consuming the research of others to being the creator of your own research.

RESEARCH

The four perspectives in this section all share a focus on research. The dissertation is the evidence that demonstrates your competence as an independent scholar, able to execute and complete a meaningful research project (See also Chapter 7.1: A Test of Your Ability). The better your understanding of research—both its abstract and practical aspects—the easier it will be for you to work effectively.

The first perspective is very abstract: Research is the creation and telling of stories about the world. These stories lie at the center of all that researchers do. Academic literature is made up of stories about the world. Not just any stories, however, but stories carefully developed using careful reasoning, argument, and evidence. The basic story that you tell is the heart of your dissertation, and keeping a focus on the basic story can help manage the complexity of the research literature.

The second and third perspectives turn to the crucial and difficult task of identifying a single question for your dissertation—a task that is fairly easy in the abstract, but that presents practical difficulties. Typically dissertation writers start from a fairly general question—a research interest—which provides a starting point for inquiry but does not provide sufficient definition to be made into a practical research project. Finding interesting questions is so easy that one often ends up with too many related but distinct research questions. The second perspective looks at how questions relate to each other and lead to other questions—to a whole web of questions related to a given topic.

The third perspective looks at the issue of defining a manageable question. To move from the whole set of questions that one can generate by considering a topic of interest and its various expressions in the research literature, to one specific question that provides the foundation for a workable research project—one that you can actually finish—there are practical dimensions to consider: what are practical considerations related to a question that will allow creation, execution, completion, and acceptance of an entire dissertation?

The fourth perspective looks at research as part of a larger community of researchers: how do you work within that larger community to create a worthwhile dissertation? Your research will be much easier to complete if you know how to use previous scholarship to define your own work.

Nothing I suggest here is independently new, but I believe the overall perspective does not get applied in dissertation writing books. The material here responds to major difficulties experienced by many of the writers with whom I have worked. This discussion is rooted in the philosophy of science—it draws on ideas expressed in the work of Karl Popper, Thomas Kuhn, Michel Foucault, and Bruno Latour (among others), especially the elements that describe the sociological character of research—because these issues are relevant in the everyday work of dissertation writers, but the focus is not on the philosophical issues, it is on the practical implications of those issues.

 The discussion focuses on issues that most scholars will recognize in their own academic community, while avoiding the abstruse and controversial.

So, for example, every scholar should be able to recognize that their work fits into and is shaped by the work of other scholars in their field (most notably the professors with whom they work most closely, but also those other sources that help define their work). More controversial positions—like the question of whether objective knowledge is possible—are not considered here because they do not provide practical guidance for a general audience.

CAVEAT: RESEARCH AND WRITING INTERTWINE

This book separates the discussion of writing and research, as if they operate independently. But they do not. You can't do research without writing. The attempt to write out your ideas as if you were going to present them to others is a valuable and effective exercise—not only does it practice your writing skill, but it forces you to reflect on your ideas with a precision and organization that is difficult or impossible without writing. When the authors of *The Craft of Research* say that "writing is thinking,"[18] it is surely this effect that they have in mind. Writing creates possibilities for self-reflection that are not otherwise possible. In scholarly writing, you attempt to explain your reasoning to other researchers, and once you put your reasoning down on the page, you and others can check it, which almost inevitably forces a deeper and clearer understanding of the relevant issues.

And as I have already said: writing and research are skills that develop with practice. By keeping the practice a unified one—a practice of writing out research considerations rather than just thinking about them—the necessary skills and products of effort support each other and help you move forward.

RESEARCH HELPS PROFESSIONALS, TOO

Professional careers require knowledgeable individuals who make good decisions based on good information. The skills of a researcher will help

---

18   Booth, Colomb, & Williams, 2008, p.14.

professionals understand situations better, and thus will almost always help them, even if they're not trying to publish research.

If you choose a professional career, you will want to be able to look at research and evaluate it, so that you can benefit from the research in your field. Psychotherapists and others in clinical settings, for example, will want to understand new treatment options; teachers will want to understand new pedagogical strategies; artists and designers will wish to understand new technologies for creation. This need to understand research is a large part of the reasoning that leads to the research requirement—the dissertation—in professional degrees. Once you do your own research, you look at other research differently.

CHAPTER 5.1
A STORY ABOUT HOW THE WORLD WORKS

At its heart, research is an attempt to understand and explain. It is an attempt to tell a story of how the world works—but not just any explanation or story will do. Research is the generation of explanations of various phenomena—stories about how things in the world behave—using methods accepted by the academic community of which you are part. The conventions of research can obscure the process of telling an explanatory story, but ultimately, all research is aimed at the creation of such stories.

The basic purpose of research is to explain some aspect of the world. Despite all the complexities of theory and method and the attempt to incorporate the theories of other scholars, ultimately the researcher needs to be able to tell a coherent story about how things in the world operate.

The story is the heart of the research project. Keeping an eye on the central story will help you create a coherent work. Even when the central story is not entirely clear—which is often the case, especially at the beginning of research—the story should be at the focus of all you do.

Many scholars with whom I have worked have struggled because they're not keeping their own story in view, but instead are spending their efforts tying to sort out differences between the stories told by others. The theories in the literature are important in helping you explain your own story, but your job is to tell your own story, not repeat those of others.

Many of the writers with whom I have worked, and many of my fellow students, struggled because they did not have good understanding of research. I have found four main reasons that many writers struggle with their dissertation research:

- They do not think they know enough to proceed (i.e., they feel they have not studied an area enough).

- They do not trust their own knowledge (i.e., they feel that there is a flaw in their understanding of the material they have covered).

- They do not know how to present their own knowledge.

- They do not understand how to integrate their work with the work of other scholars.

All of these problems can be reduced with a better understanding of research and a strong focus on telling your own coherent, evidence-based story about the world. Research is an uncertain task conducted in a context that values debate and challenges to ideas. Understanding these conditions allows scholars to make effective decisions, and especially saves the fruitless effort of seeking absolute certainty.

To get the best of your dissertation, remember that ultimately your research is aimed at helping an entire community of researchers tell a story that explains the world—a story built on evidence and sound logic, as well as on coherence with the work of other scholars.

The perspective of research presented here is very general and generally consistent with the main traditions that have shaped the culture of academia and the academic dissertation project. Therefore, these perspectives should be appropriate to almost all academic researchers, no matter their program, field of study, or philosophical/theoretical commitments.[19]

This first research perspective sets the context for those that follow: it describes a basic purpose for research. The perspectives that follow should be understood in the context of this one.

THEORY: STORIES ABOUT HOW THE WORLD WORKS.

Researchers are trying to describe the world and how things happen (or happened in the past). We can look at this as a process of creating stories

---

19 Actually, I can't think of any research done at a university that won't fit within the parameters I will describe, but as soon as one asserts that something is general, an exception will pop up.

about how the world works. Ultimately, every theory is no more than a story about how things occur in the world.

- Physicists tell stories about the behavior of objects. The theory of gravity tells stories about how objects behave—in particular, it tells stories about masses attracting each other. It explains why people and objects fall to the surface of the earth—the massive Earth's gravity draws objects to it. Other stories have explained this phenomenon of objects falling to the ground, for example, the Greek theory of the four elements—earth, water, air, fire. The theory of gravity is central to telling the story of the Moon orbiting the Earth, and the Earth orbiting the Sun, and the regular rising and setting of the sun and moon. These phenomena have also been explained as gods driving chariots across the skies. The divine chariot story is more obviously a "story," but the fact that "the theory of gravity" explains the same phenomenon as the "divine chariot" myth highlights that the theory of gravity is basically a story.

- Biologists tell stories about living beings. Darwin's theory of evolution is a story about how plants and animals came to be as they are. Again, the fact that this theory is a story is highlighted by alternative creation stories, like that in the book of Genesis. In both cases we have a story that explains how animals came to be as they are (and more generally how the world is populated with living beings).

- Psychologists tell stories about how people's minds develop. For example, Freud told stories about the conscious and unconscious; about the id, ego, and superego; and about the role of familial sexual dynamics. Piaget told stories of how people develop during their childhood. Cognitive behavioral theories tell a story of how people's emotional states are related to their patterns of thought.

- Sociologists tell stories about groups of people. Historians—obviously—tell stories about things that have happened.

- Philosophers tell stories about ideas and how to think.

- Scholars engaged in the study of literature tell many different stories. Some examine how or why a writer came to create a work, others use literature to reveal a story about social conditions, as, for example, a Marxist critic might look at how a novel reveals class dynamics.

At their heart, all theories are just stories about how things happen. When I say, "tell a story," this is not dismissive or demeaning, though in everyday language, "story" is often contrasted unfavorably with "truth" or "fact." On a very fundamental level, this is what academics and philosophers do: they tell stories.[20] Ultimately, this is what your dissertation must do, too.

RESEARCH: YOUR STORY

Researchers work to refine and/or revise the stories being told by current theories. Whatever the field, a scholar's original work stems from adding his or her own insight and evidence to the larger discourse. Research starts with a researcher's intuitive sense of a story about some phenomenon, and a sense of some flaw in that story—a blank space waiting to be filled (when someone thinks, "I wish there was research on subject X"), or an incorrect premise to be corrected (when someone thinks, "I think the story being told in the current literature is wrong").

It is this sense of a basic series of events in the world that are the anchor of all of a researcher's ideas. Whatever you work on—whatever difficult theory you engage with—ultimately you want to be able to say "yes, this makes sense as a possible explanation or description of the world," or "no, this does not make sense." You need to trust your own judgment. All your work will grow from trying to tell a coherent story about the world.

---

20   It has been argued that narrative structure—i.e., the structure of a story—is fundamental to human conceptual systems (Turner, 1996). If so, then academic work is necessarily made up of stories because it is made by human minds.

The better you can define the story of interest, the more easily you can proceed with your research. If you can't tell the story easily, it's worth the effort to try to refine it. Imagine what your "elevator pitch" would be—how you would describe your work to an interested party you met in passing. Practice writing a one-paragraph description, such as that you might submit in a cover letter or short fellowship/grant application. Such exercises can be done quickly, and they help in the attempt to refine a project.

INCOMPLETE STORIES

The stories told by research are never complete. It would be ideal to tell a complete, coherent story, but there are always gaps. It is into these gaps that most research fits. Where there are gaps, there are opportunities for research. In the sections that follow, I will discuss finding questions for research, so I will not discuss that now. But there is a two-fold importance in the researcher recognizing that research tells incomplete stories: Firstly, the scholar needs to remember that all researchers operate at the limits of their knowledge: the whole point of research is to find new understanding—new ideas that explain things not yet understood—therefore every scholar necessarily proceeds with limited knowledge: if certain knowledge were available, it would not be a meaningful site for research. Secondly, the scholar needs to recognize that even work of the best quality is rife with limitations. Good work is not free from limitations; good work manages its limitations well. Both of these points emphasize the importance of trusting yourself in the face of uncertainty: good research does not come from scholars who have certain answers, but from careful, conscientious scholars who do their best to clearly recognize both strengths and weaknesses in their work.

TRUST YOURSELF

The two preceding points—that all stories are incomplete and that research is for you to present your story—combine to provide guidance on the four common problems I mentioned above. Uncertainty is endemic to research—doubt and questions are the necessary motivation for all research. It is not comfortable to act in the face of uncertainty, but act we must. If you feel that you don't know enough, that's the nature of the business!

Having incomplete understanding of your field is not a personal failing, but rather a state that necessarily characterizes all research projects. It is true that there are many researchers who act as if they know everything and have every answer, but many people have unjustified self-confidence.

To some extent, it is necessary to believe in yourself in the face of uncertainty. It is important to trust your knowledge, regardless of its limited extent and internal contradictions. The ideal researcher maintains a balance between confidence and self-doubt, being willing and able to question accepted ideas, but also being willing to put a limit on that questioning. This need to assert something unproven is clearly expressed by Bertrand Russell: "When you are considering any sort of theory of knowledge," he wrote, "you are more or less tied to a certain unavoidable subjectivity, . . . You always have to start any kind of argument from something which appears to you to be true" (Russell, p. 37). At the time he wrote that (it was published in 1914), Russell was engaged in the general project of attempting to mathematize knowledge (he and Whitehead published their *Principia Mathematica* in 1910, 1912, and 1913). Despite his desire to set up a system of certain, provable knowledge, he acknowledged the necessity of trusting oneself—of starting with "something which appears to you to be true." Russell's confidence in asserting that one can start from something that appears to be true is in stark contrast to the work of Russell's student, Ludwig Wittgenstein, who followed very similar paths of reasoning on the same issues, but instead arrived at the conclusion that "Whereof one cannot speak, one must therefore be silent."[21] The difference in the reasoning of these two philosophers does not lie in logic, but in the confidence to assert something in the absence of logical certainty. Given the different conclusions they drew, it is not surprising that Russell was a prolific author, while Wittgenstein never

---

21 Wittgenstein, *Tractatus Logico-Philosophicus*, Chapter 7. Retrieved from Project Gutenberg (www.gutenberg.org). This single sentence is the entirety of the final chapter of the *Tractatus*.

published another work of philosophy during his lifetime. But research never proceeds with logical certainty, therefore, I encourage you to emulate Russell's attitude: trust yourself.

For those who don't trust their presentation (or who fear presentation for exposing their weaknesses), the practical response lies in remembering the endemic incompleteness of all research, and embracing the presentation as an opportunity to discover problems. Let your presentation be a tool for getting feedback that helps you understand your material better. No presentation can eliminate the inevitable incompleteness of a story; every presentation is built on a foundation of incomplete knowledge. Instead of hiding the uncertainties, the scholar boldly announces to the audience the limitations that exist, alongside any conclusions that arise from the research.

IMAGINING THE UNKNOWN

If we already knew the answer, there would be no need for research. Research requires imagination to find good questions and good answers.

Some research projects can be fully defined in terms of questions and issues set out in some prior work, leaving the researcher to generate evidence that informs us about the theory presented in the prior work. Studies in the laboratory sciences are often of this character, where research projects are deeply embedded in a research context defined by both the other researchers in the laboratory and the kinds of equipment available. At other times, however, it is necessary to imagine different possibilities for what the story could be. Some research methods, grounded theory, for example, explicitly expect the researcher to leave aside the literature and let the important story arise from the data themselves.

Often it is necessary or useful to imagine your story in terms of events in the real world rather than trying to read other people's literature: what is happening in the world? What are the causal paths? What are the possible causal paths? Can you imagine any factors that might affect what is happening that aren't accounted for in the literature?

The ability to imagine possible stories that explain the matter of interest is a crucial one. Don't be afraid of using your imagination. If you read a paper, and you think that there is something wrong in it, you may well be using your imagination to intuit the problem. If you read a paper that poses an unanswered question, and you think that you have an idea for an answer, it's probably arising from your imagination. These kinds of imaginative excursions are crucial to the development of research.

This operation of imagination is no less crucial in developing your own theories. If you recognize a gap in your own story, try to imagine different possible explanations. Stories that you imagine aren't enough for research. But once you turn those imagined stories into hypotheses and test them, you are doing research. Imagination is a crucial, valuable tool for a researcher. Thought experiments or discussion of "counterfactual" situations, which have honored places in science and philosophy, are no more than exercises in imagination—very careful exercises, to be sure, but imagination all the same. Imagining chasing a beam of light—as Einstein famously did in a thought experiment that shaped the foundations of modern physics—differs from H.G. Wells imagining a time machine or travel to the moon only in how the ideas were later developed—Einstein's in mathematical forms tested by experimentation and a community of scientists, Wells's in fictional forms limited only by his own sensibilities, and perhaps those of his editors and readers. In short, don't be afraid to use your imagination; it has a crucial place in the development of careful scholarly work.

GETTING RESEARCH ACCEPTED

In academia, research is the collaborative development of stories that describe the world. As researchers, we look to contribute our own stories to the larger discussion. We might be looking to replace an accepted story with a new one, or we may be looking to add detail to a well-known story, but however we proceed, our written work is ultimately going to turn into a description of how the world works. Part of getting your work accepted by your audience will be showing how it integrates with the work of others.

As mentioned earlier, the only clear sign of a dissertation's completeness is receiving the signatures of your committee. For the dissertation writer, and for researchers seeking publication in peer-reviewed journals or with publishing houses, the acceptance of work depends on acceptance by people from the community of researchers in your field. By understanding how others in your field decide whether work is acceptable or not, you will be in a better position to build an acceptable research project.

COMPLEX AND CONTROVERSIAL

The stories that academics tell are complex and usually controversial, so whenever we enter the academic arena, we are entering a world of competing stories, and the acknowledged and accepted goal of scholars is to test stories against empirical evidence and to embrace those stories that prove themselves by passing tests.[22] Whatever the field, there is probably some debate between the major theorists—a debate about how the world works, in some way. So, for example, in economics, a Marxist tells a story of classes in conflict, while a free market theorist tells a story of supply and demand and individual incentive and innovation. Or in psychology, a psychodynamic therapist tells a story about therapy working through transference, while a cognitive behavioral therapist tells a story of therapy working through cognitive-behavioral practices. Such debates exist in all fields, and the presence of a debate allows scholars to find issues to research—points on which the research is not clear—but these debates also require scholars to take sides—to explicitly state how their theories agree and disagree with other theories. This creates a situation where scholars can usually find support for their ideas, but choosing any source of support usually leads to choosing to disagree with those who disagree with the sources you use.

---

22 The notion that researchers should seek evidence rather than accepting common wisdom is certainly familiar. This notion that the task of the scientist is to test current theories is formalized in Karl Popper's *The Logic of Scientific Discovery*.

YOUR VIEW: CREATING ORIGINAL WORK

Your research is the story of how you see the world. Recognizing that your own ideas take center stage for the dissertation can be problematic for many because most of schooling—from elementary school to high school, and even college—is a process of other people telling you what to believe. Though questioning and individual thinking are touted as values, they are not usually encouraged, are frequently discouraged, and are too often unnecessary for academic success as long as you can repeat what the professor is saying.

When you are writing your own research, however, it is your responsibility to express your own opinions and your own perspective. You are striving to explicate your own story about the world. And you want the story to be solidly founded in reason and evidence, and also somehow new: dissertations are expected to be original work.

You need your work to satisfy the reviewers, of course. And so the story you tell should share ideas, methods, and reasoning from stories told by others in your field. The story should include details about how you define your field and about the dynamics in the context you wish to study. As noted above, there are theoretical debates on many points. In your field—whatever it is—part of your concern as a scholar will be to communicate with other scholars in your field, and so part of the story that you will tell about the world will be to explain how your story compares with other stories, and you'll also discuss how your story relies on other stories being told by other scholars. To the extent that you believe in the work of other scholars or philosophers, you will naturally have some sources of inspiration that shape how you think.

Ideally, the story that you are telling gives coherence and shape to the dissertation as a whole; and ideally, you can tell that story at various levels of detail and to different audiences in different contexts, so that you really have a good sense of the variations in how the story is told, which can help you make good decisions about which parts of the story most need to be told to communicate it effectively.

THE "MORAL" OF THE STORY

With research, the heart of the matter is the basic kernel of the story—the moral, if you will—the point the reader will learn (it is hoped) from reading—which is why a good academic work should be able to be reduced to a simple description. Such a reduction is basically what both a title and an abstract attempt: both abstract and title of an academic work attempt to convey the basic "moral of the story" in as few words as possible. Yes, there are some academic works that are not focused on a thesis to be proven, but rather on a detailed set of observations, but for such works it is the organizing principle—the reason the observations were chosen and presented as they were—that becomes the "moral" (which is why it's not really a moral of a story we're talking about—the analogy is not perfect). By contrast, in artistic, non-academic works, it is not necessarily the kernel of the story that is of interest, but the telling: reducing *Hamlet* to "a story about an indecisive man," or "a story about a prince seeking revenge for his father's death," eliminates the emotional depth that we value in fictional works. If you keep the "moral" of your story in mind at all times, it can be a huge help in writing a focused work, and focus is a big problem—especially for scholars with a lot of ideas.

If you have too many ideas, they can be a big burden on trying to finish a work. To explain the "moral" of your story with the care expected in academic work is difficult; to try to tell a story with several different "morals" is far more difficult. If you feel that you have several ideas that are important to share, choose one for your dissertation, and save the rest for other publications.

SAME STORY, DIFFERENT LEVELS OF DETAIL

Your story wants to be centered on a "moral," but it cannot be reduced to a simple statement without leaving out important detail. But which details are truly important? Context matters in choosing how to tell a story: the same story will be told differently to different audiences in different settings—these issues are discussed more later. But those contextual choices can contribute to difficulty in focusing on a single, clear "moral." To refine and focus your story and its "moral," it is a useful exercise to try to tell your story at different levels of detail. Imagine telling your story in different contexts. What would you tell a new acquaintance met at a social event? What would you tell a new acquaintance met at an academic event? What would you tell your mother? Your father? Your sibling? Your friend? What would you say if you were presenting the work to a seminar and you had 10 minutes? What if you had 20 minutes? These are thought experiments that can help clarify the choices that you will have to make in writing your dissertation. The clearer the choices, the easier it is to write.

A WHOLE STORY, BUT ALSO PART OF A LARGER STORY

Each of a scholar's works should be a whole story unto itself, but it's also important to integrate that story into the larger story told by the research community in the field. Indeed, it is expected that academic authors integrate the results of their research with larger ideas in the academic discourse on the subject. Integrating one's work does not mean agreeing with everything already published (given the controversies found in academia, no one could agree with everything). One can disagree with accepted theory while still accepting the larger framework in which the theory was developed; one can reject the answer to a question without rejecting the validity of the question.

Given that you work in a specific department (or at least with a group of departments if you're doing an interdisciplinary study), you are implicitly integrating your work into the set of theories that justified the creation of your department or program. But to be able to see the connections between your work and the other work done in your field— the ability to explicitly recognize these connections—is extremely useful both in developing your research, and in presenting it to others. These concerns of fitting a specific story (i.e., the conclusions of a specific research project) into larger sets of ideas will be discussed further in the following sections—with respect both to issues of developing research and to issues of writing about research.[23]

If you try to tell your story as part of a larger story, it will help you view the dissertation as a conceptually coherent whole, and thus you will be able to more easily bring the writing project to a conclusion.

And if you also can view the single project as contributing to a larger story into which it is integrated, then, when you try to set a limit to keep the project small, you need not feel like you're neglecting something that needs to be taught; you can feel like the limits are a necessary and unavoidable practical choice, rather than an inappropriate limitation on the work.

---

23   This is one of the areas where the conceptual work of research is most aided by the practice of writing. Trying to write out ideas forces the scholar towards a level of formality and definition that aids clear thinking and is extremely difficult, if not impossible, without a written work on which to reflect.

RESEARCH QUESTIONS 1: RESEARCH INTERESTS AND THE WEB OF QUESTIONS

Research is driven by curiosity about some story about the world. Initial motivation typically comes from a general sense that the story currently told in the research community needs to be refined—that there is some gap or error in the story. This story is the context in which you define and refine a more precise research question that addresses the question—the gap or the error—that motivated the project.

CHOOSING A RESEARCH INTEREST/AGENDA

All research ultimately starts with someone who sees a problem or gap in a story about the world that interests them and then says "I wonder about X." This main query is the conceptual anchor for what follows. But this query typically starts out in a form that is not clearly defined. The concern for a researcher is to take this question and use it to find a well-defined question that is suitable for a research project—a practical and manageable research project (a concern discussed in the next section). Almost any general question can lead to a research question suitable for a manageable research project, but finding the right question is not easy.

INCOMPLETE STORIES AND THE PROFUSION OF QUESTIONS

As previously mentioned, stories are incomplete. In every story there are boundaries and gaps, and each gap presents a question about how it should be filled, and each boundary or limit offers the challenge of reaching beyond the boundary and expanding the field of knowledge.

This proliferation of questions is both useful and frustrating—useful because it provides opportunities for research, frustrating because it does not resolve into any simple solution or focus, and, speaking pragmatically, without a good focus and defined boundaries, it is difficult to bring a project to its conclusion.

Drawing boundaries is not easy. As soon as you draw a boundary, questions arise: is it the right boundary? What exists beyond the boundary? Is something relevant being excluded? All questions like this can tempt either expanding or shrinking the boundary in order to include something crucial, or to exclude something that opens up too many difficult questions. Setting a limit is not easy; it's hard to choose to exclude something important. Limiting the scope of a study can feel like a cop-out, because it's excluding something important. Limiting the scope can often create the sense that a project is too small or too precisely focused to matter. At the same time, if a limit expands too much, or if it keeps shifting, then it is impossible to complete any research project. Completion depends on setting limits.

Research is complex and requires attention to detail. The wider the focus, the more detail that must be addressed, and thus the larger the work. A project so large that it cannot be finished will help no one. And so, research is precisely defined and limited, so that projects can be completed, even if each story is incomplete. A well defined research question helps answer questions about a larger story, and it is this that makes a project worthwhile, regardless of any limits that might make it seem like the project is becoming trivial.

DEFINING A RESEARCH QUESTION IS
ONE OF THE MOST DIFFICULT TASKS

For the research writer, defining the problem to be studied, or the research question to be answered is a problem in itself.[24] This is especially true if you have not already done many research or writing projects. The interplay of issues surrounding a question can make it hard to set a limit on research,

24   This claim parallels (and is drawn from) the claim that for design, defining the problem is the problem (see Protzen, J.-P., & Harris, D. J., 2010. *The Universe of Design: Horst Rittel's Theories of Design and Planning*. London, UK: Routledge).

especially for people who are not experienced in setting the practical limits to a research question.

Many dissertation books treat the definition of the question as a simple step that can be accomplished right at the beginning of the process. More realistically, researchers with new projects go through an iterative process of defining and redefining their subject and question in increasingly sophisticated ways by writing drafts and getting feedback. The process of turning a general question about theory into a question defining a manageable study will reveal issues that the writer did not consider at the start, thus altering the original question.

At the beginning of a project, it's usually unclear what questions can be researched effectively. For an experienced researcher who has performed many research projects, and who has that history providing a context for the attempt to define a new research project, defining a question can seem straightforward, but that appearance depends on experience from numerous previous attempts to define questions and complete research projects. Students in laboratory sciences, who typically follow the research paradigm of the professor in whose lab they work, have a much easier time defining a practical research question than students in the humanities or social sciences because they can respond to the clearly defined research paradigm that guides the work done in the lab. As I will suggest later, it is often possible for students in the social sciences to find a well-defined question by looking for questions in previous literature in their field, thus providing those students with a well-developed research paradigm. Students in the humanities have the fewest constraints on defining a question, which increases difficulty, but in the humanities one can do effective research even when the question is not entirely defined. By contrast, students conducting empirical studies—whether in sciences or social sciences—must have a precise definition of the question before they can proceed past the proposal stage. In my opinion, students in the humanities are most reliant on writing drafts to refine a focus that will serve a completed work, as they cannot as easily define their work in terms of work already done by other scholars.

FINDING QUESTIONS IN AND FROM STORIES

As stated previously, the researcher starts with a story and then finds within that story some question of interest. Questions can be found everywhere in a story, with a simple application of imagination. There are many general questions that can be asked of any story. Here are some general questions:

- "What is that, precisely?" Scholars always need to define their subject, and definition is difficult. In the study of their own field, most scholars have seen how different authors present different definitions of the same concept. The concept of "intelligence," for example, is defined in many different ways ranging from the view that created "IQ" tests, to the different types of intelligence suggested by a variety of authors, such as Goleman's "emotional intelligence" or Gardner's eight different types of intelligence.

- "How do you know that?" Academic work requires evidence of some form; it is not enough to simply assert the truth of a claim. This general question can take many more precise forms for a specific research project. It can be asked from a historical perspective: where did the claim come from? It can be asked from the perspective of evidence: what evidence is there? It can be asked from the perspective of accuracy: is the claim really true?

- "How does that work?" Every story includes causal relationships (i.e., A caused B), and we can question any such relationship. If someone says that the moon rises because it is orbiting the earth, we can ask: how does it orbit the earth? If someone says that the moon orbits the earth because of gravity, we can ask how gravity works. If someone says that gravity works because of the curvature of spacetime, we can ask how spacetime becomes curved (and we may ask what spacetime is, too—because we want scholars to be able to define their terms so that we can understand them). Or, for example, if someone says that a psychological state arises from learned experience, we might ask how people learn or how people experience. If given some neurological answer to that question, then we might next ask how neurological systems work, and so forth.

- "What actions might we take, if that is true?" If we say that the moon orbits the earth, for example, we might ask whether we can travel there, and what that would require. If we know that psychological states arise in certain ways, we might ask how to create or eliminate those psychological states, depending on whether they are beneficial or detrimental.

- "How does that connect to this other thing?" Stories have limits—beginnings and ends—and therefore we can always ask how the story relates to something that was not included. To follow the questions about the moon, we can ask whether the sun is also orbiting the earth, or if some other relationship holds? Or we can ask: how does the psychological state we're studying relate to other psychological states? Or, will the psychological dynamic observed in the original study operate in the same fashion for some different population?

- "Is there is some alternative to the accepted story?" Science and scholarship progress, in part, through the willingness to challenge dominant theories. Usually, accepted theories have weaknesses or flaws that motivate the search for an alternative theory. For example, the notion that humans are rational decision makers long held dominance in Western thought, but people saw flaws and developed challenges, so that a person observing the literature can find one or more challenges to the idea that people are rational decision makers. In some fields—philosophy and critical theory, for example—the debates are widely recognized. Whenever you are working with an accepted idea, you can ask whether there is an alternative explanation—either one reported by some author you have read, or one that you imagine yourself.

It is very easy to find additional questions. Any claim can be questioned in many different ways. The fact that it is easy to generate questions, however, does not mean that it is easy to define a question that will be a good foundation for a research project. This multiplicity of questions can be a big problem when different, closely related questions begin to compete for attention. A good research question will have good practical limits that make completion possible, and a good research question will be connected to and derived from the current research literature in the field. These two ideas will be discussed in the next two sections.

Recognizing the dissertation as one preliminary approach to your questions about a larger story—a first try at answering those questions—makes it easier to keep your project small enough that you can finish it. By seeing the dissertation as only one small contribution to a larger program, you won't feel like you're cheating yourself just because your dissertation isn't a wide-ranging magnum opus. Instead, you can see the dissertation as the necessary first step towards the fulfilling career that you intend—which may include writing a magnum opus, if you so wish. Then you can set achievable goals, get it approved, and get the degree. And then you can go on to pursue your interests as bearer of a degree that lends weight to your words.

RESEARCH QUESTIONS 2:
A MANAGEABLE QUESTION

In order to bring research projects to completion, the crucial step is to identify a research question that defines a manageable project. No matter how crucial or interesting your question, if it doesn't lead to a completed project, it doesn't help you or anyone else. Setting practical limits for a small project is more effective and more valuable than pursuing some grand project that will never be completed.

If you would rather finish a project than wander around exploring ideas, it is important to make decisions that set limits and otherwise define the project so that it is practical and manageable. In the previous chapter we looked at how different ideas interweave and lead to new questions, and thus how one can find different questions that contribute to the understanding of some larger issue. Now we look at questions with the focus on the pragmatic issues that influence the project's outcome.

By doing a good job of defining your research question, you will be more successful in carrying out your research. Choosing a limited question that allows you to complete a project is not a cop out; it is the first step a reasonable researcher takes in approaching any big question.

THE DESIRABILITY OF A SMALL PROJECT

Most scholars are driven by a large question or large set of questions about major ideas or issues. To be motivated and interested usually requires a sense of importance or value for the project, thus the value in having a large question of importance. But a single research project ought to be planned so that it can be completed and shared with others: The research community does not benefit from a scholar's unfinished project, and a scholar who works endlessly on a single unfinished project has nothing to show for his or her labors. Given this context, adding in the practical limits faced by a graduate student (with respect, especially, to time and money), and acknowledging the theoretical inevitability of some incompleteness, the benefits all weigh in favor of making projects smaller so that they can be completed quickly.

For those who want to get out of school and on to a professional career, the benefit of completion and the corresponding career advancement are usually compelling enough to motivate a smaller project. I have, however, sometimes worked with people who said "Since this is my last chance to be a student, I want to do special work." Such a position is not inherently wrong—we all have to make the best choices for our own lives—but getting your degree doesn't stop you from doing further research, while delaying your degree to do a larger dissertation project does prevent you from progressing in a professional career of the sort that calls for an advanced degree.

In laboratory sciences, the pragmatic nature of research design and publication are readily apparent: students work in a laboratory supervised by a professor, on the professor's projects. The larger research question that guides the lab as a whole is broken into a large number of more specific research questions, each of which will be examined in a different study. In this setting, students become involved in writing and publication of multiple works that are all part of a larger agenda, and in that process, they see how other scholars set practical limits on the scope of a specific manageable project.

Students in the social sciences and humanities don't have the same close interaction with and participation in a developing line of research, and thus they don't have practical experience in seeing a larger question broken into smaller manageable research projects. In the social sciences, students may only see empirical studies through the lens of published work, and published studies are often significantly different from the kind research that a student can practically accomplish—a limitation largely related to the fact that employed professors who have had the time to develop grant funding typically have far more resources available than do graduate students. In the humanities, where no set of experimental data constrains the work, the difficulty of limiting a project is perhaps worse, because there is always the temptation to add another data set to further confirm or develop a theme.

Questions are not easily constrained, but for practical reasons we want them to be. Part of the task of the dissertation writer is to be able to take an initial research question and define it sufficiently so that a reasonable set of data and analyses are used to generate a set of useful insights on which they can report. Part of this will require identifying questions that already exist in the literature, or questions that you have about the literature, so that you can compare your work to other material in your field.

In setting limits, there are generally two classes of concerns to address: those that are directly related to the research project, and those that are external to the project itself. I will briefly discuss the latter first

EXTERNAL CONCERNS

In defining a research project, there are practical dimensions that are contextual, rather than directly a matter of the question itself. The interests, strengths, and weaknesses of your professors, for example, are external to any specific research project you choose, even though those interests, strengths, and weaknesses will significantly influence the ways in which you work together. Another external concern is intellectual fashion: it is easier to find support for an idea that is currently of interest to many; the more people who have interest in an idea, the easier it is to find people to work with and sources of funding. Such external factors should influence your choice of a project, especially if you are deciding between different options that all interest you.

In choosing an area of research for your dissertation, you might consider:

- Your knowledge of the subject and the literature on the subject. All other things being equal, it's better to work on a dissertation project in an area that you know well: The better you know the area, the less extra literature review you will have to do, and the more quickly you can finish.

- Your future career. Different projects will lead to different opportunities and thus can influence your career. Ideally the subject that offers the best prospects for your career will also offer an opportunity for a good, manageable research project.

- Your institutional context, especially your professors. Any choice of interest naturally aligns you with the professors who have similar research interests/agendas. Choice of subject affects your choice of professor and/or your relationship with your professors, and possibly the availability of other resources.

- Your interest in the subject. Dissertations take hard work for months or years. Following something that is not interesting for a long time can be torture. The greater your interest in a subject, the more you will appreciate your work, and the more you will be motivated to stick with the subject through the problems that arise during research. This relates to choice of career: do something that will help keep you motivated. I view your interest as external to your question in the sense that a well-defined, practical question may be of interest to one person and not to another. I would say that this is the most important external factor: don't sign yourself up for a project that bores you.

All four of these concerns will influence your experience in writing your dissertation. It is to be hoped that you can find a subject that has all these factors in its favor. If there are conflicting factors (e.g., the subject you know and like best would lead to working with a bad professor), there may be no clear best choice, but at least asking these questions can help make a good decision.

INTERNAL CONCERNS

There are two key concerns in choosing a good research question that are matters of how you define the question itself: a connection to existing research, and manageable dimensions.

Connection to existing research

Research is not done in isolation; rather it is a community endeavor. All scholars work within a matrix of ideas that have been defined by those who have come before. When Sir Isaac Newton commented that he was "standing on the shoulders of giants," he spoke for all researchers. When you view the world, your view is, at least partly, through the lens of concepts that you have learned from others. Part of your responsibility as a scholar is to acknowledge the sources of your ideas; the better you can explain the sources of your ideas to others, the better the chance that your work will be accepted.

Beyond this responsibility to acknowledge your influences, are the opportunities presented by making connections to previous research. A good connection with prior research can help you in two practical dimensions. First, it can help you define your question more precisely: the more closely your project aligns with other published research, the easier it is to set limits and define concepts, because you can follow the limits and definitions used by the research that influenced you. Secondly, a good connection with other research will help make your work appear acceptable to your professors and other readers. I have seen that many students struggle with their schools' explicit expectation that a dissertation include a "theoretical or conceptual framework," not understanding that "the theoretical framework" is basically just the story about the world that your research question is working with— either refining or challenging—so showing how that story is connected with or derived from the literature resolves this concern.

Connection to Prior Research, Convention, and Originality

Dissertations are supposed to be original work, so some people think that they can only be original by diverging from previous literature as much as possible. But this is unnecessary and creates more difficulties than it resolves: it separates your work from the support of the literature to which it hopes to contribute. It is, perhaps, counter-intuitive, but having the proper connection to existing research will facilitate originality rather than stifling it. Originality need not be massive change; valuable originality can often be found in making only one small change to a prior framework. If you have truly radical ideas, I would not suggest that they be squelched. But you are making choices for your life: keep the practical dimension in mind. If your professors support your radical ideas and you can finish quickly, great! But if you want to challenge convention, including your professors' beliefs, it might make sense to pick a dissertation topic that is not directly confrontational and to delay the challenge until you have your doctorate.

Choose Your Battles

If you have to challenge a theory that is dear to your professors, you can always look for a specific disagreement with that theory and then try to build a research project focusing on explicating and supporting that specific disagreement. Thus, for example, if you wanted to object to Free Market theory while working with a Free Market professor, you might have better luck focusing on one specific claim of the theory—the assumption that humans are rational decision makers,[25] for example, or the assumption that rational actors making rational decisions will lead to socially optimal outcomes[26]—rather than trying to reject the entire theory. By focusing on the specific claim, you can leave aside the larger debate—in this example you need not say "Free Market theory is all wrong," you can say "this specific claim utilized by Free Market theory is wrong," and that can make all the difference in the world with respect to the kind of response you would get from a Free Market advocate. In such a situation, you can develop a dissertation that agrees with many things that your professors agree with, while still maintaining a productive working relationship even while working on something they might oppose.[27]

---

25   This assumption pervades modern economic theory—it is central in the work of Adam Smith—but it is also an assumption rejected by a good deal of research, including the work of Daniel Kahneman and Amos Tversky (mentioned earlier), which won a Nobel prize in Economics.

26   An assumption made by Adam Smith in *Wealth of Nations* in the famous "invisible hand" passage, which has been often disputed and refuted, as, for example, in Garrett Hardin's famous work "The Tragedy of the Commons."

27   Within reason, of course. Some professors are not going to entertain ideas that differ from their own, no matter how well connected to the literature.

Manageable dimensions: Setting practical limits

Practical limits help you finish your work. Some questions may be more emotionally compelling than others, but if they require significantly more work, they're not good candidates for dissertations. As mentioned in the previous section, it should be possible to find a small slice of a bigger question—a slice small enough that you can finish the project in a reasonable time.

If we can recognize a small project as serving a larger research question, we can define a dissertation project small enough to be quickly completed, without feeling like we're compromising the quality of our research or abandoning the larger issue that motivates us.

Finding a good question is difficult, and the difficulty may seem to be compounded by consideration of practical issues. But extra effort in finding a good and practical question is typically rewarded by finishing sooner.

Smaller Is Better

For many of the scholars with whom I've worked, one of the great difficulties in creating a manageable question is the disappointment related to how limited its scope is. We all want to do something that's meaningful, and many feel that by cutting the question down too much, the work loses significance. My response is to remind them (and you), that if it's well done and well positioned with respect to other research, a small question can be very meaningful. Remember, too, that no matter how good the question, your research won't be very meaningful to anyone else if it is poorly executed, incomplete, or both.

Manageable Data Sources

Another issue in finding a manageable question is the availability of data. In conjunction with thinking about subject matter, think about what data you can gather. Different research questions call for different types of data and analysis. Questions that you find in the published literature may require data sets that are beyond the practical scope of a dissertation writer. As you begin to refine your question, consider what kinds of data might answer the question, and whether you could get that data. Additionally, you can think about the question in the opposite direction: if there is some source of data that is readily accessible (for example a dataset generated by one of your professors or some other publicly available data set), you can explore questions that the dataset could inform.

Some data are simply easier to gather than other. Data sets generated by other researchers provide an opportunity for meaningful analysis beyond that done by the original researcher without requiring that you gather your own data. But such data sets may be difficult to integrate with your own work if the premises that generated the research don't match your ideas. When working with human subjects, some groups are much easier to work with than others. College students (especially psychology students) are often used for research because the professor who is also a researcher (or a teaching assistant who is also a researcher) has access to the students and has power to schedule their time. It is more difficult to gather data from a group of adults who are unaffiliated with the university: people are busy and don't always want to offer their time. And it is much more difficult to gather data from children because of bureaucratic barriers set up to protect experimental participants, as well as the resources necessary to recruit and schedule them as participants.

Resource Availability

Speaking more generally, it is important to plan using a reasonable assessment of your basic resources—your time, your energy, your money. The same project that is eminently practical for a professor with research resources available is a bad choice for a student without such resources. If, for example, you want to do a study involving human participants using computers, a relevant resource is the number of computers that you can access: if you have access only to your own personal computer, it will be much harder to carry out such a study than if you have access to an entire computer lab.

Another resource to consider is time: a project that requires a year to get results is a far greater commitment than a project in which results can be gathered in a month or two. A botanist friend of mine once told me that he worked on mustard plants because of their short reproduction cycle—he called them "the fruit fly of botanical research," referencing the common use of fruit flies because of their rapidity of reproduction—and he told me of an acquaintance of his who researched corn, and for whom the loss of one crop meant the loss of a year because of issues related to the propagation of the corn in the right circumstances. If you are interested in social sciences, it is inherently more time consuming to do a longitudinal study (one that examines changes over time), rather than a cross-sectional study (in which two or more groups are compared at a single point in time).

Tight Focus

Limit yourself to talking about one idea, and work on it carefully. Don't let the one focal idea bleed into related ideas, and if you have more than one idea, save the extra ideas for future projects. In addition, keep the number of examples to the minimum necessary to demonstrate your ideas. If you're doing an empirical study, you're limited to gathering the data outlined in your proposal, which helps limit the analysis as well. For scholars working from archival data and literary sources, the limits are not so clearly defined: in the initial definition of the project, it is easy to overestimate how much material can be used successfully, and during the process, it is tempting to add additional sources for review. Keep your focus tight to keep your project to manageable dimensions.

Methodology

Your choice of method affects the practicality of a study. Some methods are largely dependent on choice of material to be analyzed: a student of literature or a historian analyzing archives, for example, typically uses less formal methods than a social scientist doing an empirical study. In cases like this, limiting the material to be examined is more important then changing the fundamental method.

In social science settings, I have heard it argued both that quantitative research is easier and that qualitative work is easier. Both views are overly simple: doing good work requires effort, regardless of method. Qualitative methods are easier in some ways: it can be easier to define and propose a qualitative study, because qualitative methods often presume less knowledge going in (and, in the case of methods like Grounded Theory, prior knowledge of a field that might prejudice the researcher is discouraged). This greater ease of project definition is balanced against a more lengthy and open-ended analytical process once the data are gathered. Quantitative methods require more preliminary setup: for a good quantitative study, the parameters of the study—the variables of interest, the data instruments, the data analyses—must be fully defined before beginning, so the proposal task is more difficult than for a qualitative method. But this initial difficulty is balanced against the relative ease of completing a quantitative study once the proposal has been completed—since the analyses are already planned before the data are gathered, the final analyses can usually be carried out quickly.

I would discourage mixed-methods studies. In terms of the potential quality of results, mixed-methods studies are great. Practically speaking, they involve all the difficulties of multiple different studies, in both setup and analysis. The author of a mixed-methods study must do all the work for a quantitative study, and all the work for a qualitative study. For a dissertation writer who wants to finish quickly, a mixed-methods study is generally a bad choice.

SUMMARY

Defining a workable research question usually means limiting the scope severely. As previously noted, this can be disappointing if you feel like you are abandoning an important large question in favor of a minor point, but the simple anodyne for that is to remember (1) that the smaller project is a necessary step contributing to the larger project, and (2) finishing a limited project is better than chasing a grand goal for years.

CHAPTER 5.4
THE LARGER RESEARCH DISCOURSE

So far, I have spoken of research from an individual point of view: the attempt of an individual scholar to define a research project that helps explain the world. But research is a community activity concerned not only with the discovery of understanding, but with its dissemination as well. As a researcher, all your work is done within a web of ideas built up within a research community. Understanding how to place your work in that web is crucial to the effective use of literature and the effective definition of a research question.

As previously mentioned, academic questions are shaped by the use of common theories. To define your basic concepts you will almost always rely on the work of others. Your research questions will typically arise from perceived gaps in the literature. Your own vision—your own story about the world—should be your primary guide, but your ability to link your work with the larger scholarly discourse is crucial.

Creating links with other research does not require agreement with other research. A link to other research can be created by contrasting your ideas to those previously expressed. Research depends on a willingness to challenge and test accepted knowledge. And, as you are probably aware, what counts as "accepted knowledge" in academia depends on whom you ask. You are probably aware of debates within your field between adherents of different views. There are few points on which there is universal agreement; there are far more that are hotly debated. This is good; it creates an opportunity for you to contribute to your field. In creating your own research, this diversity of opinion and published literature provides the framework in which your own research develops.

FOLLOW YOUR OWN IDEAS, BUT RECOGNIZE AND ACKNOWLEDGE THE SOURCES THAT SHAPED THEM

From our childhood, school teaches us that there are right and wrong answers and that the right answers are those that the teacher expects. We are taught that there is a basic story that is true. In college and in graduate school we may be exposed to the various debates that abound in academia, but because of the habits of accepting ideas from our teachers, we may not view the diversity of theories as evidence of the struggle to develop good theories—the struggle of the researcher—instead we may view these diverse theories only as material that we are responsible for knowing, without thinking how this literature relates to our own ideas. The habit of accepting professors' opinions does not serve you as a researcher because as a researcher, you have a responsibility to test theories and to accept only those that stand up to your tests.

Do you automatically think of the things taught in school as the best theories available? Do you accept them unquestioned, as some form of truth? Several philosophers have argued that science is only the best set of theories we have at present; knowledge is determined not only by objective fact, but by political, historical, and cultural accident.[28]

Your work as a scholar fits within a community made up of many different voices, all working together to form a consensus picture of the world. If you are writing a doctoral dissertation, you have been steeped in this culture for years, so much so that you are likely to think in terms of some theory formulated by some scholar, but you may not even recognize the source of the idea, or you may take it for granted that everyone knows who was the source of the idea.

---

28   Michel Foucault and Jacques Derrida are famous exemplars of this claim, but citing them brings in a politically loaded context. But it is worth noting that Sir Karl Popper, whose model of science is fundamental in most empirical research, and who still argued for a form of objective knowledge, also includes such contingent elements in his description of science (see his *Logic of Scientific Discovery*, for example). Thomas Kuhn's *The Structure of Scientific Revolutions* also follows this basic premise.

Many who observe the social processes by which "truth" is generated (e.g., Foucault) reject the notion of objective truth, but to Popper, at least, the role of the community of scientists does not eliminate the possibility of an objective truth.

For this book, with its focus the basic context of academia, such fundamental theoretical debates need not be decided. But as a scholar, it is useful to know where you stand on such issues, because knowing your position will allow you to connect your work to other scholars in your field who also take the same position.

If you can tell your story and cite the sources for its different elements as you go, you will fit your work into the larger discourse, and this will help you reach your audience who, presumably, are scholars involved in the same discourse to which you are contributing.

As I mentioned previously, many dissertation writers get stuck thinking, "I need to include theory in my dissertation," because there is an explicit statement in their school's dissertation guide or dissertation template that calls for discussion of "theoretical background." In response, writers often try to apply some tangentially related theory to their work in some awkward way. But the entire discourse surrounding you is theory. If you can tell your story, and cite the sources for its elements, you will have included theory by default.

THE "HIDDEN" STORY IN ALL RESEARCH

The story of your research is the central story about the world that is the subject of your dissertation. But parallel to this story about the world is another story that you will need to tell to best reach your audience. This is the story of your ideas: where did they come from? How did you test them? What evidence and reasoning support them?

A research work is not, of course, a memoir of a research project (e.g., "when I started this project I believed X, but I came to believe Y"), but it does present the history of how the idea developed (e.g., "This study looked to test the idea X; the results of those test ultimately suggest Y;" or "Author A claimed X, which became the starting premise for this research.").

In presenting your work, it is important to show both the story about the world that interests you, as well as the story of how your inquiry and conclusions were founded.

THERE ARE MANY VOICES

Academic literature is filled with disagreement and debate. This diversity helps you define your work: with whom do you agree and disagree?

Chances are, no matter what position you take, there will be those opposed. By acknowledging the different sources that shaped your thinking, you become part of this debate, and, in a way, you also insulate yourself from it.

Many writers struggle when they worry about people rejecting their points, but by aligning your work with that of others, you gain allies and support for the ideas you use. It's best to take it for granted that someone is going to disagree. If you align yourself with a given idea, those who disagree with it will attack you. But by explicitly acknowledging the source, you can often short-circuit questions by saying: "my source is debated by some, but that debate is outside the scope of this work." It's a tactic that doesn't always work, but often does. If, for example, you're using Marxist theory, someone stridently opposed to Marxist theory might attack any statement drawing on Marx, but most professors who don't accept Marxist theory, I think, would be inclined to read your work with the attitude that as long as you are consistent with Marxist premises, you're fine.

ASSERT YOUR OWN VOICE

As I have said before: you need to trust yourself. The dissertation is supposed to be an original work. You cannot simply repeat what is told to you by others. This is true even if your dissertation chair wants you to slavishly follow instructions: even in following instructions, there will be need for you to make crucial theoretical choices. The dissertation depends on your vision, your guidance, and your way of understanding the world. Write what you believe. Explain why you believe what you believe. Build the entire project around how you understand the world. Don't be ashamed to assert what you believe, but at the same time, understand that academic work calls for evidence and reasoning to back up beliefs.

Whether you plan an academic or professional career, you will struggle to find your way unless you believe you have something valuable to add. Any career in an intellectual field requires independent decision making. For both dissertation and career, it's important to learn to trust your own voice and your own reasoning, and to be willing to share that reasoning with others, even though they might criticize it.

USE OTHER VOICES TO MODEL HOW TO ARGUE

While you do want to assert your own voice, remember that your job as a scholar does not rely solely on you expressing your ideas about the world; it also relies on others understanding the arguments that you create. You are not speaking to yourself. By looking at what others talk about, and looking at how others speak, you can shape your own words so that they better reach others. What kinds of points do they pursue? What kinds of points do they leave unexamined? Do these practices seem appropriate to you? Not only do you want to examine the theories of scholars to see if you agree with them, you also want to examine the way scholars build their arguments. Such examination will allow you to model the methods of supporting and developing an argument that seem most convincing to you.

ENGAGE IN DIALOGUE WITH OTHER VOICES

Build your writing around a conversation with the ideas in the discourse.[29] Talk to the ideas that you agree with: Explain why you agree with them; talk about whether those ideas can be expanded to areas that the original author didn't extend them to. Talk to the ideas that you disagree with: Explain why you disagree with them; explain why, despite their problems, they are worthy of consideration; explain how you would modify or replace them. The dialogue with other ideas is the process by which our understanding develops—both individually and communally. Challenging, modifying, or even rejecting the ideas of another philosopher does not imply disrespecting them: using an idea shows that you believe it is worthy of attention, even if flawed. Of course, for practical and political reasons, it makes sense to try to build a positive dialogue with scholars that you disagree with, rather than trying to base your work on the rude rejection

---

29 A book written for college students, *They Say/I Say* (Graff & Berkenstein, 2007), does a very nice job of discussing this point and describing how you can build your work in dialogue with other scholars.

of their work. It is typically possible to do this because for disagreement between scholars to be meaningful, they have to share at least some of the same reasoning structures, otherwise they wouldn't be part of your field of study. Therefore, it is usually possible to find a point of agreement that allows you to start the dialogue with any theory with a statement like "The idea defined by the author is a good starting point, but . . ."

Because of the diversity of voices, you will almost inevitably disagree with someone if you hold your own position, but this does not mean that you have to focus your work on the disagreement.

SUMMARY

Your story is drawn from the larger discourse, and it contributes back to it. The more clearly you recognize where your ideas come from—those drawn from the literature, and those that are the product of your own imagination and work—the more easily you can create a work that will be understood and accepted by your audience.

CHAPTER 6:
WRITING

A dissertation project is not just the generation of original research, it is the written expression of that research. The demands of writing differ from the demands of research, and being able to see the writing as writing—an attempt to communicate ideas to other people—provides practical guidance.

WRITING

"I can't start writing; I need to do more research." I've heard many writers say something like that, as if writing is something that only happens after all the other research work is done. It's a nice, simple strategy: research first; write it up second. Unfortunately, it's not effective. As I have already suggested, research and writing can't be separated (a point that I don't discuss in detail, but that is implicit in much of what I say about the practice of writing). Additionally, writing itself is a skill that improves with practice, so writing now will help you write more easily in the future. And still further, the task of writing itself—the attempt to communicate ideas—has elements that take time to develop independently of the research.

The two perspectives in this section look at practical matters of writing a dissertation. The first perspective focuses on the dissertation as a piece of writing: What does a written dissertation look like? The second focuses on the dissertation as a writing project to be completed: How do you use your resources effectively?

These perspectives step away from questions of research and subject matter. Looking at your dissertation as a writing project focuses attention on important practical concerns that are not always given conscious attention, especially questions of how to write productively, how to write better,[30] and, perhaps most importantly, how to complete your work.

Some important perspectives on writing that are covered in other books on writing—for example, what writing habits and practices work, how to set up a writing space, or how to punctuate—are set aside in order to focus on some less frequently discussed issues.

---

30 Of course, the most significant contributor to improving your writing is practice, as I have mentioned previously.

CHAPTER 6.1
A PIECE OF WRITING
TO BE COMPLETED

One concern for the writer is with the form of the written work to be created: what makes up a dissertation? And how can be it be done so that it is well received? When one thinks of writing in terms of the attempt to be heard and understood, many of the issues that frustrate writers— punctuation, grammar, structure—make more sense. If your goal is to get your dissertation accepted and completed, your task is facilitated by having a clear sense of how to write so that you meet your audience's expectations.

As I have said, it is not enough to have good ideas; completing a dissertation requires communicating those ideas to others. It is necessary, of course, to do the intellectual work well—and writing drafts is an important part of that process—but in addition to the research is the task of sharing your story with others in a way that they understand and accept. By understanding the rhetorical concerns—the concerns of persuading your readers—and by keeping these concerns in mind as you proceed with your research and produce your written drafts, you will work more effectively, and thus will be able to get the best responses with your work. The concern of this section is to get you to think about the design of the written work: how will it engage the audience? what is it going to look like? How long is it going to be? What material will be included, and what material will need to be cut? This section is not a blueprint or template for a finished work, nor is it focused on the process of writing, instead it is concerned with issues that will come up in the process of research and writing, and that will influence how your work is received.

THE FACTS WILL NOT SPEAK FOR THEMSELVES

A fact can be right before our eyes, and if we do not have our attention drawn to it and its value, it may remain unnoticed and/or unappreciated. It is your job as a scholar to speak for the value of the material that you are presenting. It is not enough to simply put forth a list of facts; it is necessary to explain why they are interesting and why they are significant.[31] And when your audience is made up of busy, opinionated people (which professors typically are, and I mean no disparagement), getting their attention can be difficult. The conventions of research, of course, play a crucial role in reaching them, but so too do the tools of persuasion.

In the Platonic and Aristotelian traditions, rhetoric, or sophistry, is frowned upon in contrast to reason, and there is no doubt that rhetorical devices can be used to mislead or deceive: an *ad hominem* argument, for example, will suggest that one should judge the truth of a statement in accordance with one's judgement of the speaker, rather than focusing on the truth of the statement itself, but this is not how research is supposed to proceed: statements are supposed to be judged according to their own merits.[32] However, the fact that rhetoric can be abused, doesn't mean that it can't be used productively, too. You may gather wonderful data that leads to ground-breaking conclusions, and you may still benefit from thinking about the rhetorical dimension of your work. In speaking for the data you have gathered, you need to explain their significance, and that is facilitated by understanding how to convince people that things are significant.

SPEAKING TO YOUR AUDIENCE

It goes without saying that you want your audience to understand and accept your work. Many factors influence this goal. The reasoning of your research ought to be the most important factor in being understood, but there is also the rhetorical concern: how do you reach an audience? Rhetorical concerns

31   Which is rather more difficult than simply saying "This is interesting and/or significant."

32   Realistically, we all often judge the truth of a claim according to its maker; it is practically necessary: this is the lesson of the story of the boy who cried wolf: it takes effort to check the veracity of someone's statements, and someone with a history of lying doesn't motivate that effort.
   Even in academia, such conflation of idea with speaker is practically unavoidable, and often useful. By calling on the reputation of a published author we can avoid the attempt to prove every statement we make: that is the role of citing the research literature.

include dealing with the practical details of writing—organization and flow of ideas, sentence structure, grammar, spelling, and other stylistic conventions—and they also include issues of focus: choices about how to frame the work, especially its scope, motivation, and significance. It is with these last choices that the author can integrate considerations of the audience's interests and needs. When thinking in rhetorical terms, the writer asks, "who is my audience, and how can I reach them and convince them of the value of my work?" By taking this perspective, the scholar begins to consider not just the focal issues of the research, but the contextual factors that influence the presentation of that material.

You need to convince your audience that your work is worthy of their attention and effort. Your professors have an obligation to read your work, of course, but counting on that obligation to get a fair reading is a risky proposition: professors are notoriously busy and there are plenty of students who haven't gotten the attention that their enrollment status would justify. Just because your professors owe you their attention, doesn't mean you'll get it. You may have followed your course of research because you found it interesting, but that's not going to necessarily motivate a reader to engage with your work. Instead, you have to consider what will make the work interesting to another person. Saying "I think it's interesting," might work, but that's not very compelling to a scholar surrounded by a large body of literature, all of which claims importance and interest.

Instead, you want to frame the work with respect to things your audience will value—other research, in particular. If an author poses a question in a published piece, there's a good question that working with that question will interest that author. Widely read works provide good context, because you know that people are interested in the work to which you are responding. Additionally, you want to present the work so that the reader believes that you know what you're doing. Common forms and expectations—grammar, style, etc.—are important because correct or incorrect use of such things can convince a reader that you are or or not competent as a researcher, even though these common forms are not in any way dependent on a researcher's ability to do research.

AUDIENCE AND EXPECTATIONS

Reaching an audience depends on understanding their interests and expectations. With a dissertation (or thesis, or work submitted for publication), satisfying the expectations of the reviewer(s) is the sine qua non of acceptance. Many of the expectations of an academic audience are determined by standards of research, and these standards influence matters of presentation, leading to many of the conventional forms that can be observed in the academic literature. There are expectations related to the specific type and context of the work—for dissertation writers, these expectations are implicitly set out by the dissertations previously accepted in their program.[33] There are also the more common standards related to writing—grammar, punctuation, and style—that are designed to make reading easier.

It is not necessary to slavishly follow conventions or expectations. At times, there may be very good reasons to violate a convention or expectation. But every time you choose to violate a common convention or expectation, you should do so with the expectation that you will be challenged for that choice. Therefore, if you want to violate some convention, do it consciously and for reasons that you can explain. With respect to matters that arise from your research, it is to be hoped that you have reasons for any deviation from convention.

SCOPE AND SIZE OF PRESENTATION

One aspect of writing to your audience is to fit your work into the scope expected. Whatever you're presenting, if you come close to expectations for size and scope, your audience will be more accepting. Presenting a work that is significantly shorter than expected may lead to questions of why the work isn't longer; presenting a work that is much longer than expected may lead to complaints that the work is too long (or related complaints that the work isn't sufficiently focused).

---

33   Lovitts sets out to make these concerns explicit in her work: *Making the Implicit Explicit* (Lovitts, 2010). Of course her work is general and cannot incorporate the specific expectations of any specific program.

As I have already mentioned, any story can be told with differing levels of detail, allowing presentation of the same main ideas in varying lengths. Both the dissertation project, and the written dissertation itself, involve telling the same story at different levels of detail at different times. As mentioned earlier (and in the next section), a dissertation's title, abstract, and introduction all tell abbreviated versions of the story that the entire dissertation tells in detail. For all of these, you want to try to conform to general expectations.

Speaking strategically and pragmatically, planning your writing is aided by understanding the expected scope of your work. To this end, it is useful to use dissertations done by students who have completed your program as guidelines for the length of your own work. Depending on your program, the expectation for a dissertation might be somewhere between 100 and 300 pages. In the UK, there is a generally codified expectation that a dissertation will be about 80,000 to 100,000 words, which translates to about 250-300 pages.

The type of work influences the length: a quantitative study will typically be shorter than a qualitative study, and most work in the social sciences will be shorter than work in the humanities.

Once you know the expected length of the final project, it is easier to proceed. A good strategy for early drafts is to aim at a draft that is 50% of the final anticipated length. Such a strategy helps keep focus tight, and reduces the effort involved in the earliest drafts. If you submit a short draft that is accepted, that's great, and if you are told that you need to add more material, it's usually much easier to add material to a draft than it is to excise material.

SAME STORY, DIFFERENT LEVELS OF DETAIL (PART 2)

The same story needs to be told in different ways and with different levels of detail depending on the circumstances. But whatever the context, the key is the underlying story. The clearer your vision of the underlying story, the easier it is to adapt it to different lengths. At the same time, every attempt you make to tell the story, and to tell it in a different context, contributes to increasing the story's clarity.

In your dissertation you will tell the same story with four different levels of detail:

- The title should tell the crucial elements of the story in one or two phrases.

- The abstract will need to tell the entire story in about 300 words.

- The introduction and conclusion will both try to tell the whole story in about 5 to 25 pages (this will vary depending on the nature of the work).

- The dissertation as a whole will need to tell the story in extensive detail in maybe 100 to 300 pages.

If you have a coherent story to tell, and if you can tell it well at many different levels of detail, you will find it much easier to communicate with those whose help you solicit while trying to complete the dissertation—from recruiting committee members, to applying for grants, to filing routine departmental paperwork.

CONVENTIONS, INCLUDING GRAMMAR AND STYLE

It's easy to get frustrated with conventions like grammar and style, which can feel insignificant compared to the central argument of the paper. But these conventions in writing are largely driven by the practical concerns of readers; the conventions are intended to help readers understand, and thus, when your focus is on reaching your audience, these conventions take on a greater value.

The purpose of writing is to communicate. If we are writing to present our research, then the ideal response from our readers is that they focus on the issues that matter to us, and they understand and respect our reasoning. It is no fun at all to give a work to a reader who then focuses on other matters—

whether some tangential issue that you did not consider, or "minor" issues like sentence structure or formatting. Of course, if a reader complains about sentence structure, we can't easily tell them it's not important, because their response shows that it was important to them. While responses that focus on flaws or matters we had left aside might be useful feedback for making our work better, they are not the most useful feedback that a researcher can receive if there are still questions about the research itself.

Most of us are taught grammar and spelling as a set of "rules" that we have to follow, typically in a context where someone will correct us, and even chastise us (in the form of lower grades) if we fail to follow these rules. Such punitive contexts focus attention on following the rules without ever really explaining why those rules arose in the first place. Rules of grammar and spelling developed to serve a practical purpose: they ease the communication between reader and writer. If you're reading a work, and the author uses an unconventional spelling—"smoak," for example, instead of "smoke"[34]—it can be distracting or even confusing. And misplaced punctuation can alter the meaning of sentence, also creating confusion.

But dealing with these conventions can become easier with practice. Earlier, I used the driving of a car as an analogy for writing: when we start driving, the basics—managing the steering wheel, transmission (even automatic), turn signals, etc.—demand our attention, but these concerns fall away with practice, allowing us to focus our attention on where we want to go. This analogy is useful for thinking about the experience of a reader, too: the conventions of writing—spelling, grammar, and style—are like the controls of the car: we get used to them, which allows easy use. If, in driving, the controls are suddenly moved, our attention is diverted from the main task of getting where we want to go—suddenly our attention is needed just to locate the proper control. By parallel, when a reader is presented with unconventional spelling, grammar, or punctuation, their attention is diverted from the subject matter. For a writer who wants readers to focus on the ideas, this is an undesirable result. The value in the stylistic conventions is in making it easier for your readers to follow your main ideas without distractions.

---

34   In Laurence Sterne's *Life and Opinions of Tristram Shandy, Gentleman*, this spelling of "smoke" is used.

PRESENTATION: INTRODUCTION, DEVELOPMENT, AND CONCLUSION

The purpose of the written work is to reach people and convince them, at least, that the research was clearly reasoned and competently done, or better, convince them of the correctness of the conclusions. But most scholars I've known have focused almost exclusively on the material to be presented, and in the effort to organize the ideas, they give little attention to understanding their audience and how to reach their audience. It is, of course, important to get the basic story in order. But the academic writer cannot only focus on the philosophical issues; the academic writer must also be a storyteller. Your audience has interests and expectations, and if fail to meet those expectations, your work will not get the reception you desire. I have already suggested the practice of thinking about how you would tell your story to different people in different contexts as a valuable exercise when planning your dissertation—a crucial part of that exercise is trying to imagine what the audience wants and needs.

While it is hard to generalize across audiences—different people want different things—there is a basic pattern that all audiences face: there is a moment of time at which they first make contact with a presentation (whether written or oral); there is a time that they receive the bulk of the material; and there is a time at which they leave the work.[35] Each individual may move through these phases at different paces, but the basic structure is unavoidable. This pattern provides some pragmatic guidance for writers. The basic ideas are simple and familiar to most, but these ideas, which are not given much attention by many writers who struggle, can provide exactly the kind of guidance that can assist an author.

Introduction

In any presentation, some of the work should be dedicated to attracting the reader. The beginning is the crucial moment for most works: everything follows

---

35   When things go poorly, there is very little time between the audience making first contact and the author leaving the work. This is partly why the abstract and introduction are so important: a bad abstract that dissuades further attention will obscure a high-quality work.

from catching the reader's attention. No one wants readers to look at their abstract and immediately judge the work unworthy of attention. For this reason, I believe that the most important pieces of a work are, in order, the title, the abstract, and the introduction. A good title will bring the readers to the abstract. A good abstract will bring the reader to the introduction. And a good introduction will inspire the audience's attention for the work that follows.

What are the practical implications of this view? The writer wants to be able to introduce the subject in a way that the reader understands and thinks sufficiently important and interesting to warrant further attention. Admittedly, your professors have a responsibility to read your work whether they think it's important or not, but surely it's better to have them interested.

Typically, an introduction starts with a wide view, setting up a context for the focal material. The context will present a general vision of some area of interest, and then will focus in on the matter for the rest of the work. The introduction will want to make the general context interesting, and will want to show why the chosen focal material is important in that context.

There are two distinct contexts to which the academic writer needs to attend in writing an introduction. There is the context of the work with respect to the world, and there is the context with respect to the academic discourse. It is important to be able to say "this work matters to the world in the following way . . ." And to say "this work is valuable in the research discourse in the following way . . ." For example, in describing the importance of a work on pedagogical theory, one might say (1) that the pedagogical theory is valuable because it will help students learn better, and (2) that the pedagogical theory and its investigation are motivated by interests expressed in the research literature (these interests might be expressed implicitly in the literature, e.g., as some gap in the literature). Or, as another example, a work of history would be motivated both by the value of understanding history, and by some limit or failure in the scholarly literature.

The Body

The bulk of your writing—the body of the work—is primarily a matter of presenting and organizing your material. In the body of the work, there is less concern for rhetorical matters, in the sense that if you have succeeded in gaining your readers' attention, they are then waiting for you to present the material that was promised in the abstract and introduction. But rhetorical concerns do not disappear: there is still the need to help your reader see the ways in which details relate to the larger argument. Within a large work there are internal divisions—the sections marked out by chapter divisions and section headers—and each internal division benefits from the basic rhetorical structure described above: introduce an idea and present its context before moving on to details of the idea, and then provide a concluding statement that recapitulates the context. Within the body of the work, an introduction to a section will want to define the relationship to three aspects of the context: the overall story arc, the material that immediately precedes it, and the material that will follow.

The Conclusion

The conclusion will work in a fashion opposite to the introduction: it will move from the specific conclusions made in the body of the material, to speaking about how these conclusions fit into a larger context. A conclusion will recapitulate the main conclusions and the context that motivated the research, and then look at how the larger context is altered by the new conclusions or new data. The larger context, again, has two aspects: the main subject matter, and the academic discourse on that subject matter. For many dissertations, especially those in social sciences, it is common for a conclusion/discussion chapter to include sections on "implications for future research" and "implications for policy/practice." While humanities dissertations do not always include explicit sections for such concerns, to the extent that the work is motivated by some motivating idea, the conclusion is called on to address the ways in which the research results impact our understanding of that idea. The conclusions drawn from the research and their relation to the original motivating idea are, in a sense, the "moral" of the story that I discussed earlier.

COMPLETENESS/INCOMPLETENESS

Previously, I have argued that all stories are incomplete. This is true when we're thinking about how ideas relate to each other and how to begin and end a story. A certain inevitable incompleteness arises from putting our ideas on the page: we must start with some idea, but that idea might itself require explanation, and we must end with some idea, but that idea might have unexamined implications. We have to start and end somewhere, but we can't discuss all the ideas that relate to our starting and ending points, so there is always some incompleteness.

To take a completely different angle, we might argue that all stories are "complete" in the sense that the telling of the story begins at some point, and ends at another. If you are presenting orally to an audience, the story begins when you start speaking, and ends when you stop (or when the subject moves away from your story). If you are presenting in writing, there will be a first page and a last page, and (unless it's a one-page work) pages in between. The audience starts to listen or read at one time and then stops listening or reading at another. One of the tasks of the writer is to manage the incompleteness of the theoretical story in a way that its presentation feels complete: this is a matter of presentation and choices of how to direct the reader's attention; it is not a matter of answering all possible questions or addressing every related detail.

SETTING LIMITS

Written works have limits. Every written work has a final page; no written work includes everything. As I note above, it is important to know the scope of the work that you are trying to create: what are the expectations in your program? 50,000 words? 80,000? Whatever the number, you, as the author, must actively choose what stays in and what gets cut.

I find that it is useful (and often necessary) to say "... but that is outside the scope of this work." Given that the scope of your work is largely up to you (in consultation with your professors), you should not be afraid to set the limits that you wish. If you say "that is outside the scope of this work," you set up a situation in which you acknowledge the existence of issues worthy of discussion, but you tell your reader that these matters are excluded by choice.

The phrase "but that's outside the scope of this work" is of great practical value in helping keep your work focused. If you're trying to create a short early draft (which I recommend), being able to say that something is outside the scope of your work is an invaluable tool.

Your readers may not always agree with your choices, but then if you have a wide audience, chances are that someone will disagree no matter what you say. No writer needs to please everyone. Dissertation writers need to please a very small group of individuals. If your professors (or other reviewers) ask for development of some idea, then you need to take that request seriously. But, as I suggested earlier, it is easier to add material to a short draft than to remove material from a long draft, so start with a shorter draft, and don't be afraid to leave some material outside the scope of your work.

DON'T DEFEND YOUR BASIC ASSUMPTIONS

A key point in limiting your work is to avoid defending your basic assumptions. Trying to defend basic assumptions can lead to wasting a lot of effort on material that is too general. I read works that dedicate paragraphs or pages to explaining an obvious motivation—educators who spend paragraphs arguing that it's good for students to get better results, psychologists who spend pages giving reasons that people shouldn't suffer depression, and so on. But such arguments should be unnecessary: an educator shouldn't have to argue that it's important for students to learn, etc. Such basic premises should be asserted not defended, so that the more precise and focused project can receive attention—the educator can talk about the specific educational issues, etc.

When basic assumptions are more hotly contested intellectual points, it's even more important to assert them rather than defending them, because the defense can be extensive and inconclusive. A literary critic using, for example, post-colonial theory, doesn't want to extensively defend the value of post-colonial theory before they conduct a post-colonial analysis of some text. An attempt to justify the general value of post-colonial theory and defend it against all attacks could take pages and pages, fail to convince the doubters, and not even touch on the specific points that the critic wanted to discuss.

Even with more specific topics, it is necessary to assert a starting point that doesn't need extensive defense: an examination of treatments for a specific pathology (whether psychological, medical, or other) ought not spend extensive time arguing the pathology is properly defined—that the pathology is defined in the literature is enough of a starting point, even if some people debate whether it is a pathology or not.

Defending basic assumptions can be a large project that keeps you from your own research. If your work all derives from examining the implications of some controversial assumption, then the defense of that assumption is entirely outside your work. If you have derived that assumption from the literature, then you shouldn't have to defend the assumption beyond citing your source, no matter how controversial.

An example in my personal experience was a writer developing a distance-learning program for evangelical Christian colleges. Such a project depends on the existence of evangelical Christian colleges, and without that starting point it is impossible to proceed to suitable distance-learning programs. The value of such colleges, however, is contested in the scholarly literature, and the author with whom I worked had dedicated 75% or more of the dissertation draft to defending the existence of evangelical Christian colleges, while distance-learning programs were hardly addressed. By expending so much effort on a debate that was the starting point of the work, the author failed to address the real subject.

If your research is intended to address a specific controversy (e.g., whether there should be evangelical Christian colleges), then, of course, it is necessary to address and acknowledge that controversy in some detail, but with limits! But if all your work follows from accepting the controversial claim (in this example, the interest in developing a pedagogy for evangelical Christian colleges only follows from accepting the assumption that such colleges are worthy), then you ought to simply assert that claim. If you're concerned that someone will ask about the debated issue, you can assert the assumption in a qualified fashion. One says, for example, "In developing this pedagogical program, it is acknowledged that many question the value of evangelical Christian colleges, but that debate is outside the scope of this work." Or, speaking abstractly, one can say: "Although X is widely debated, this work accepts that claim." Speaking generally, although you want to look at a wider set of ideas to give context and motivation to your work, you don't want to spend extensive time arguing points that you accept.

SUMMARY

No piece of work is perfect, and no story is complete. But that doesn't mean that you can't finish your project. You can certainly turn in a draft that addresses all the necessary points, and also acknowledges its own limits. When writing, set a target for your length, and keep an eye on the rhetorical concerns: what needs to be done to introduce the idea? What needs to be done to develop it? And how do you draw your presentation to a close? By using practical and rhetorical guides, you can set limits for your written drafts, and by setting limits, you can finish a work and turn it in.

CHAPTER 6.2
COMPLETING
WRITING PROJECTS

In addition to thinking about the forms that help you reach readers, there are also the concerns of how to set up a writing practice and the management of a writing project. Managing a dissertation-length work is a significant undertaking. Good practices will facilitate your efforts.

As previously discussed, the dissertation project as a whole includes and involves a whole series of writing projects—from the first proposal draft, through necessary administrative descriptions of your research and other work presented as you go, to the final dissertation draft. Each of these writing projects is significant in its own right. The better each one is written, the more likely it is that people will receive your work well, and lend their support accordingly. From small to large, each writing project shares some basic characteristics. There are additional concerns with the dissertation (and sometimes the dissertation proposal), due to the greater size.

THE BIG PROJECT AND THE SUB-PROJECTS

The writing of a dissertation is a large project whose ultimate aim is a written work. Along the way, you will need to write drafts and other smaller pieces—prospectuses, progress reports, etc.—that also need to be completed and submitted. It is a platitude to say to take things one step at a time, but with a project like a dissertation, it is more effective to focus your writing efforts on the next small step, than to think too much on the details of the final work.[36] As you plan your larger project and your

---

36   I emphasize "details of the final work" because every piece you write should be looking to tell the whole large story in some way. Even when you present small pieces of your research, it's important to be able to frame them in terms of the larger project that motivated them.

research, you want to keep your eye on the large issues and the overall management of the project—and it can be useful to write notes and try to work out plans on paper. But with respect to times that you sit down to write, focus your attention on the next piece—the next step. What is the need for that step? What is the rhetorical structure of that step? How long does it have to be? Who is the audience? And so forth. In the end, of course, each chapter of the dissertation needs to work with the other chapters, but as you go, keep your vision on smaller pieces: What does this chapter have to accomplish? What does this section of the chapter have to accomplish?

LEARNING AS YOU GO

One reason that it is useful to focus on one piece at a time is that you learn so much as you write. For me, the experience of writing is a bit like the experience of trying to teach a class: unexpected questions arise—in class because some student asks, and in writing because I have the opportunity to reflect on the ideas I have just expressed and on whether the expression I've used does justice to the idea. There is a common trope that fiction writers start to feel that their characters "come to life" and, once put into context, suggest possibilities that hadn't occurred to the author before. I feel this matches my experience to some extent, even though my writing is focused on ideas, not characters: as I write, the ideas themselves suggest possibilities that I had not previously considered.

As a research writer, it's to be expected that you'll learn a lot about your subject and come to a deeper and subtler understanding of your material as you work. This is especially true when working with unfamiliar material. Every time you write a new draft, you are faced with the challenge of stating your ideas (which requires understanding of the ideas) and then with asking whether you are expressing your ideas well.

The more you practice expressing your ideas—and the more the new paper resembles something you have written before—the easier it is to plan what you want to say for the entire work ahead of time. But often, even if you start with a good vision of what you want to say and how you want to say it, you may find as you go that there are problems with your plan, or that there is some alternative course of action that is obviously superior. Even if you can clearly see the whole work before you, you'll probably be better served by being ready for some trial and error: write a draft and see what you learn from writing it, and then write another draft.

Whatever you're writing, it's good to start the writing project with the attitude that your first draft is more a test run than an attempt to create a final project. Plan for your first draft to be a mess—the first draft is about learning. If you are willing to explore with early drafts and then rewrite later, you'll be able to focus on your ideas and the main points that you want to express without getting distracted by things like grammar and spelling, and without dismay if some better plan of action occurs to you as you work. As I already suggested, you will benefit greatly from practice. The skill that develops with frequent practice (i.e., frequent rewriting) is the reason that, ironically, those most willing to rewrite copiously are also those who can often generate a good first draft that needs little revision. Over time, the willingness to revise and rewrite lead to a practice that develops skill as a writer.

KNOW YOUR SCOPE; USE THE SCOPE TO AID IN PLANNING

As mentioned previously, you should be aware of the size of comparable works. When planning writing and making outlines, it can be very useful to consider the expected length. Pragmatically speaking, I recommend aiming at a draft that is 50-75% of the expectations. Pick a number of pages or a number of words that will be your target, and then, when making an outline, try to plan that outline with respect to the total pages that you are planning on writing. This exercise can be extremely useful in helping make a draft feel manageable.

When thinking about writing a 100+ page work, it's easy to feel overwhelmed. Most dissertation writers have never written anything that long, so it seems like an intimidating project. And it's not really possible to keep all the details of 100+ pages in clear focus at once, so it feels like a difficult goal. By creating an outline that divides the work up, and sets page (or word count) targets, you can transform the large, intimidating project into a series of smaller, manageable pieces.

Example 1: if you are planning a quantitative empirical study, and your dissertation target is 100 pages, then you might start with an outline that aims at 75 pages. This outline will typically have five chapters: introduction, literature review, methods, results, and conclusions/discussion. If these are divided equally, that would mean 15 pages for each chapter. You may never have written a 75-page paper, but I'll bet that you, as a doctoral candidate, have written a 15-page paper. So looking at a series of 15-page chapters is typically less intimidating than thinking about the full 100-page dissertation. Realistically, the chapters of an empirical study won't all be of equal length, but still to work from an outline that says to write a 10-page introduction, a 25-page literature review, a 5-page methods, a 15-page results, and a 20-page conclusion/discussion is much easier than to simply try to write each of those chapters without guidance to length.

Example 2: Not only can we break the dissertation up into chapters, we can do to each individual chapter what we did to the dissertation as a whole: break it up into smaller pieces with pre-defined targets for length that make the work easier. For a dissertation in the humanities—literature, for example—we might have a final target of 250 pages (roughly 80,000 words). A literature dissertation might be broken into chapters each dedicated to a different author, or chapters dedicated to specific works, or to specific themes or analytical approaches. We might, then imagine a literature dissertation as having five chapters: an introduction (20 pages), three body chapters (70 pages each), and a conclusion (20 pages). For a first draft, we could aim at 75% of those targets: 15 for the Introduction and Conclusion, and 52 for each body chapter. Using those targets, we have three 50+-page first-draft chapters, which is still a pretty intimidating project, but each of these can be outlined and broken apart, too. Each chapter will have its own introduction and conclusion, which provide the transitions from the previous chapter and to the next chapter, and which tie the chapter in to the larger fabric of the dissertation. And each chapter might then include a number of internal sections. If the work is dedicating each chapter to a specific author, we might dedicate sections to different works, which might give an outline for the chapter that has five parts: introduction, analysis of work 1, analysis of work 2, analysis of work 3, and conclusion. If we try to split up the 52 pages of the chapter on this outline, we might get the following split: introduction (5 pages); analysis 1 (14 pages); analysis 2 (14 pages); analysis 3 (14 pages); conclusion (5 pages). Again, this kind of division transforms a work of intimidating length (52 pages) into a series of works whose lengths are well within the experience and ability of the typical graduate student.

AIM FOR BREVITY

Pragmatically speaking, it's usually less work to write a shorter draft. I suggest aiming your drafts—especially early drafts—at a fraction of the expected total. There are five additional reasons to keep your draft targets short:

- If you write a short draft and it's accepted, then you have moved more quickly toward completion.

- As I mentioned earlier, it's typically much easier to add material to a short draft than it is to remove material from a draft that is too long. When adding, what is needed is to find a place to insert the material, which can often be done without significant revisions to the rest of the draft. When removing material, however, it may be necessary to rewrite large portions of the work in order to remove material that is intertwined with the larger body of the work.

- In my experience, it is much more common to over-shoot a length target than it is to come in under it.

- There is greater psychological ease in aiming for a shorter target: it is both easier and less intimidating to work on a shorter paper.

- It's better to be brief and leave your reader wanting more than to overwhelm your reader with material. If nothing else, a short work gives your reader fewer opportunities to find that you have made a mistake. In general, the absence of some specific issue from a well focused work is less likely to cause a reader to doubt your abilities than an overabundance of material that is only tangentially significant.

REMEMBER YOUR DISTANT DEADLINES

I assume that you know your deadlines well enough to submit work on time. That's not really what I'm talking about. Rather, I'm talking about working in a way suited to the distant and unfixed deadlines for dissertation submission. When taking an exam, of course, you know exactly when the deadline is—it's the end of the exam. And it's a very firm deadline—you can't typically talk your professors into giving you a one-day extension on an exam that you've already started. And so you write what you can. You do the best you can, and at the end of the exam period, you turn in what would certainly be judged a mess in another context. But it's not another context, which is the point. Most people have turned in a one-draft wonder—a paper written with no revision, and usually with no time left on the clock (or even after time had expired, because it's pretty easy to negotiate a one-day extension on a paper). Again, this might be appropriate in some contexts—last minute paperwork, or something that came up on short notice.

Most of the writing projects that support a dissertation are not like this. Usually, you have as much time to work as you want. This can often lead to procrastination, as the urgency of the work is less than the immediate demands of life. It is pretty easy to put off working on the dissertation because of immediate demands of teaching or a job or of family. If you develop a regular practice that balances work on the dissertation with other things, the lack of an absolute deadline won't cause problems, and you'll be able to turn in work with a suitable degree of polish. Use your time to accomplish the various tasks that support good writing and good communication. Take advantage of the time you have to write multiple drafts and to revise multiple times.

With large works, the last minute things that work with a seminar paper of 20-30 pages become overwhelming, especially compounded with the sense that such a work deserves a greater degree of care than an exam or other short-term work. And, if you get caught in such a situation, instead of trying to get a one-day extension, you end up paying registration fees to enroll for the next semester. By keeping an eye on distant deadlines, you can save yourself stress, time, and money. This is all obvious, in a way. But I repeat it because it fits in with my general suggestion of writing daily.

WRITE EASILY; WRITE AND REWRITE

It should be noted that it is virtually impossible to avoid writing several drafts. Think of it this way: how likely is it that the very first draft you turn in will be accepted as is? Chances are that even if you're absolutely brilliant, the draft will get sent back for proofreading and final formatting. More likely is that the first draft gets sent back with suggestions for content development—such a request by a reviewer is no point of shame—it's hard to get everything perfect on the first try. Early on in the process, just try to get your ideas onto the page in whatever form you can. The time for refining and editing a draft comes a little later.

One popular book on writing that I appreciate, *Bird by Bird* (Lamott, 1994), makes an explicit point of emphasis on "Shitty First Drafts," with a chapter dedicated to (and titled for) the subject. Another book, The *Clockwork Muse* (Zerubavel, 1999), discusses writing four drafts of each work as a method of increasing productivity—a claim that undoubtedly sounds paradoxical if writing feels tedious. An extreme example of rewriting can be seen in an interview with Hemingway: "How much rewriting do you do," asked the interviewer. "It depends," answered Hemingway. "I rewrote the ending of *Farewell to Arms*, the last page of it, thirty-nine times before I was satisfied."[37] Hemingway was only talking about one page, of course, but the point here is not to threaten you with the need to rewrite things thirty-nine times, but rather to suggest that productivity and good writing spring from a willingness to dive in, make mistakes, and then try again.

---

37   Quoted in Bolker, 1997, p.100.

Chances are, you'll really benefit from writing several drafts of your dissertation, not to mention any ancillary material describing your dissertation and dissertation work (e.g., prospectuses, proposals, year-end progress reports, etc.). The need for rewriting can be frustrating, but there really is no substitute for writing and sharing your work with other people if you want to produce a complete work. From such attempts to express yourself, you'll learn what works and what doesn't. If you embrace the need to write, and decide to write easily and voluminously, you'll create an atmosphere that encourages this process of writing and revision. By "easily," I do not mean without effort; rather I mean "without worry about making mistakes." "Easily" speaks about attitude, not level of effort.

Write fast; write so that you can have time to revise. Write without concern for punctuation and grammar. Write as an activity to discover hidden aspects of your ideas. There is time for punctuation and grammar once you've gotten the ideas out into a workable form.

CHECK AND CHECK AGAIN

Proofreading helps. It saves time, effort, and hassle, because your audience will probably complain about minor errors, even if your main ideas are in order. If you have troubles with grammar and punctuation, get someone to help.[38] You want the reader's attention to be focused on the ideas and on the research; if there are too many minor errors, the reader will at least be distracted and at worst be prevented from understanding you.

Following on the previous point, I want to emphasize that the first concern is to produce the work and to get your ideas on the page. Getting the ideas down is the starting point. But once you have the ideas down, go back and review the work; try to clean up whatever you can. In the first stages of creating any draft, you want to get ideas down in any form so that you can learn from them; in later stages, as the time to submit to someone else approaches, concern will shift to getting the details worked out.

38　While it is unethical to have someone write your research for you, there is no such ethical concern with hiring a proofreader.

The construction of the draft should be done without care for these formal concerns—as I suggested in the preceding section, it's good to write easily, focusing on the ideas, and not concerning yourself with making a clean draft. The careful revision and checking for proofreading and grammar is best accomplished as a task unto itself, a task that is only wanted immediately prior to submitting the draft to a reader/reviewer. Indeed, until the absolute final draft—the one that is going to be filed with your school—you want to minimize the proofreading effort in accordance with what you know of your audience. If your professor is going to complain about punctuation, it's necessary to proofread. But if your professor will accept minor errors as a natural part of the process of writing, then you can minimize your proofreading.

PRACTICE REGULARLY

I know I devoted significant attention to the importance of working regularly, so this essentially a repetition of ideas mentioned earlier, for which reason I will be brief. Write and rewrite. Write and then edit. Practice writing ideas if you find an idle moment—anything is better than nothing. But most of all, practice your writing regularly. Create drafts. And learn from the experience.

At the same time, don't over work. Writing is difficult and requires a fresh mind. Write for a few hours a day. Spend the rest of the day in other pursuits. The evidence suggests that the most productive writers generally are not trying to write for the entire day, but they do find some time to write (e.g., Boice, 1990).

SUMMARY

The ultimate goal is to submit work that will be accepted. If you recognize the practical acts that lead to a complete draft, and carry them out, you'll be able to generate complete drafts, even in the face of uncertainty.

CHAPTER 7:
PROOF OF INSTITUTIONAL ACCEPTANCE

Another crucial perspective is that of the dissertation's place in the institution: if dissertations are not simply a rite of passage or some device to torture you before you receive your degree, then what are they for? Issues of research and writing—the discovery and communication of ideas—do not explain why the university asks students to write dissertations, nor do they give any guidance for dealing with individuals within the institution whose intentions might not be entirely benevolent.

INSTITUTIONAL CONCERNS

The dissertation isn't just a search for understanding (i.e., research), and it isn't just a written report of your research. It's also what you have to do to get the institution to accept you and accredit you.

The final two perspectives are concerned with looking at the dissertation's role within the institution. Why do universities have students write a dissertation? What does the institution get? What do institutions want? Universities want (among other things) prestige and accreditation. Part of how they get these things is through producing graduates who do things expected of good students. Universities use dissertations as a test to ensure that you are sufficiently competent in your field that you are worthy of the accreditation you will receive; this is part of what they do to ensure that they will continue to be accredited themselves.

If the dissertation is a test of competence, what are the traits being tested? This is the concern of the first perspective in this part. The relevant traits, generally speaking, are those related to competence in your field, including knowledge of the literature and theory in your area. Other traits that are important are more generic expectations of students and scholars: the ability to envision, design, manage, carry out, and report on your own research project. But the dissertation is not only a test of these traits, it is also supposed to help teach them, which, indeed, is one of the worst problems with dissertations, in that it is awkward to test something that has not yet been taught.

The second perspective focuses on the relationship with your dissertation committee members, as well as any other professors who are gatekeepers to your advancement. Ultimately, the institution does not judge you; ultimately, the institution assigns specific professors to judge you. Knowing that people will judge your work, you can begin to consider how your relationship with those people will affect their judgment of you and your work (many aspects of this perspective apply to working with any audience—e.g., editors, review boards, candidate search committees—not just professors). But beyond their role as judges, your faculty can be of great help with the research and writing—they are supposed to *teach* after all—if you can get them to help. What can you do to foster a productive relationship with your professors, so that your professors can help you achieve your goals?

CHAPTER 7.1
A TEST OF YOUR ABILITY

The dissertation is a test of your ability—the final test given by universities before granting doctoral degrees—and it is also an exercise meant to develop skills and abilities. So what skills and abilities is it supposed to develop and test? The better you understand what the university is looking for, the better you can get the developmental benefit the project is intended to have, and the more easily you can fulfill the desires and expectations of the university's representatives—your professors or reviewers.

It would be silly to ignore the fact that the dissertation is done to get institutional approval: if you want the degree, you have to satisfy the institutional expectations. While there are cases in which conventions and institutional expectations are put aside, getting around conventional expectations is work in itself. For the moment, let's focus on the conventional expectations.

The dissertation is obviously a test of your ability. It is the final step in achieving the doctoral degree. But what is it testing? I've heard many complain that the dissertation is about jumping through hoops—meaningless tasks to please arbitrary whims—but is that really believable? Do you believe that administrators and teachers sat around asking "what are meaningless tasks that we can assign students to ensure that they suffer as much as we did when we were students?" I've heard that basic idea many times from many people. I don't think it's plausible. I'm a cynic—I believe that people often act for the basest and most selfish of motives—but even I don't believe that professors are generally trying to dole out suffering. Yes, I believe that some professors are sadists, but I can't believe that there are enough sadistic professors to explain dissertations as the product of sadism. I absolutely believe that many professors are selfish, self-centered egotists who generally disregard the needs of others, but such people wouldn't plan to force others to do meaningless work, if only because that would create more work for the selfish professor him or herself.[39] Despite my cynicism, I know many professors who have good intentions, who really want students to succeed, and who make sacrifices to help their students. In fact, despite my cynicism, I believe that the great majority of professors are people who really want to teach others for all the best reasons.

In this chapter, I ask: if the dissertation were designed as a well-intentioned teaching exercise, what would it entail? Here are the leading issues, as I see them:

1. General familiarity with research in your field

2. Command over your subject area

3. Competence in reasoning

4. Ability to manage and complete a project on your own

Each of these is reasonably important—"reasonably" in the sense that it's not silly that you would be asked to be able to do these things to show your achievement as a scholar. The doctoral degree, after all, is an award for accomplishment as a scholar—what would it better test than these things? It is true (as I will discuss in the next section) that the dissertation might alternatively be viewed as a negotiation with your committee in which the only factor of importance is satisfying them, but that's only one perspective. These four points on which the dissertation might test you are basically the same skills that will help you in any career that an advanced degree would further—after all, are you really in a good position if you have your degree but you still can't do scholarly work, or make productive use of the research literature in your chosen profession?

---

39   In similar vein, I believe that there are professors who are in over their heads, who don't really understand research, and who create needless work through incompetence. In my experience, these are few, but even the best, smartest professors make mistakes at times.

FOR FUTURE PROFESSIONALS

Yes, you may never need to carry out another research project on your own, but you certainly should have familiarity with the research in your field, command over specifics subject matter relevant to your work, and competence in reasoning. You may not have to carry out your own research projects, but in fields requiring advanced degrees, it will be necessary to have sufficient understanding of research that you can respond to new situations. For example, healthcare professionals may need to research treatment efficacy, especially when faced with an unfamiliar diagnosis or treatment option. An educational administrator might be required to evaluate novel pedagogical programs. An architect or engineer might want to research new construction technologies. In many or most fields, the desire to use evidence-based practices leads to a need for professionals who are able to follow changing ideas about the field by reading scholarly literature. When faced with novelty, professionals need to do research, too. The experience of having carried out research will change how you look at it and both facilitate and deepen the value of working with research literature.

GENERAL FAMILIARITY WITH YOUR FIELD

Naturally, institutions want their graduates to have a good working knowledge of their fields. But this should not be the main purpose of the dissertation.[40] Other requirements of most doctoral programs—oral exams, course work, etc.—develop and test general competence in your field. However, as already discussed, any piece of scholarship belongs to a larger discourse of scholarship. Making your dissertation a good piece of scholarship will involve fitting it into this larger context, and that is largely an exercise in understanding how to frame your specific questions within the larger context of the field in which you study. Doing this effectively requires significant familiarity with the general field.

---

40   While general competence should not be the job of your dissertation, you will benefit if you can convince your faculty committee of your general knowledge. If your faculty committee believes in your command of your field, it will help you get the dissertation approved. But this is more of a concern for the next chapter with its discussion of working with professors.

You should not be using the dissertation for lengthy explorations of aspects of your field not directly related to your work, but the introduction should partly include an attempt to delimit your work against a wider background.

COMMAND OVER YOUR SUBJECT AREA

Similarly, it is not surprising if your institution expects you to be familiar with the important research that is directly related to your own research.[41] Of course, if you look at research as part of a larger discourse, then this will naturally come as part of your work: you will position your work with respect to important ideas that are shaping the discourse concerning the issues that you want to illuminate.

Part of having command over a field includes being able to make good judgments of what needs to be discussed and what can be left out of the discussion. Having command over a field does not mean exhaustively showing that you have closely read everything; it means showing that you have read things, and that you can make good judgments about what is important and what is not. This kind of judgment is integral to, and naturally flows from, developing your own voice.

To some extent, like general knowledge of your field, this command over your subject matter is something that the institution has other ways of testing—exams, written and oral, for example—so it should not be the primary concern of the dissertation.

A COMMON PITFALL

One problem that many writers have is trying to write too comprehensive a literature review. If you try to show every piece of literature written relevant to your subject, it is really hard to get on to doing your own work, because there is almost always another idea around the corner. Hopefully you can leave the

---

41 Again, this should not be what the dissertation is for, but if your faculty committee believes that you have command over your area of specialization, it will help.

demonstration of command over the larger subject area out of the dissertation.

Both general familiarity and command over the specific subject are woven into the very fabric of good scholarly writing, even when the focus of the writing is kept as tight as possible on the specific research questions that shape the project.

In any event, I recommend keeping drafts of the literature review as short as possible to avoid getting lost in relevant literature that has little immediate significance for your research. It is much easier to set limits in terms of number of pages or words than it is to set limits in terms of relevance.

COMPETENCE IN REASONING

Part of commanding a field of knowledge and developing an idea for a research project in that field is being able to build competent arguments that explain why you take the positions that you do. But a more general skill is desirable as well. Speaking generally, competent reasoning means that you are able to think through things and give better explanations than "because," or "I believe." Faith is accepted in religion, but in academia and professional contexts you are expected to build your arguments on stronger foundations. At the very least, you are expected to be able to support a claim by pointing to others who also accept that claim.

People respect those who show their work and reasoning clearly. So being able to explain why you have reached a position can lead to getting respect. There are times when you just have to assert a position without defending it in detail, but you don't want to rely too often on such unexplained positions.

Of course, you want to reason effectively. If you use modes of reasoning that are not accepted—if you mistake correlation for causation, for example—or make other common mistakes, then you are likely to meet resistance. Therefore, you want to make sure that the way you build your arguments recognizes important rules of logic. The best way to learn these things is to practice them by explaining the reasoning you use to reach a conclusion, not just the conclusion itself. The dissertation is both an exercise to help develop skill in using the tools common to your academic discipline to support your reasoning, and a test of whether you have done that successfully.

ABILITY TO MANAGE AND COMPLETE A PROJECT ON YOUR OWN

This is a tremendously difficult and important aspect of the dissertation. It is probably the one for which you have had the least preparation. As previously discussed, most of school is a process of answering the questions of others and repeating back what you have told. But with the dissertation, you have to make all the decisions about how to move from topic to topic and from premise to premise.

If you are in one of the laboratory sciences, chances are good that you have plenty of role models working through their own experiments, so you have a chance to work with people struggling with the same kinds of project management issues that you are. A student in a lab may well have participated as co-author in a number of projects while working on their own dissertation. But if you're not in a laboratory science, there's a good chance that you never really have an opportunity to get insight into the working processes of other researchers, and so your attempts to manage your project may be uncertain.

To a large extent, the management of a project involves all the perspectives that I discuss in this book. One of the major hurdles that dissertation writers face is getting stuck looking at the dissertation as something akin to research papers that they have written earlier in their career as students. There is a kinship, but the kinship is limited due to the many different dimensions of the dissertation project that other projects don't involve—other projects don't involve the same lengthy period of work; they do not involve the same extended search for a good question; they do not involve satisfying multiple professors. Most papers that you write before the dissertation are much more limited in scope. To finish your dissertation, think of the dissertation as a project that needs to be managed. If you can finish the project, you will have successfully navigated the test.

THE TEST IS ALSO THE LEARNING EXPERIENCE

Because research projects are slow to develop—especially for those engaged in their first independent project—the test and the pedagogical experience are intertwined: you learn to manage independent research as you go. It simply isn't practical to expect a student to spend a year or more doing a dissertation-scope project as an exercise in learning to write a dissertation, and then to spend an equally long period having the same student write a second dissertation as a test. Not only is too much time spent that way, but if a student is able to complete the "training exercise," there is already proof enough of the student's ability to complete such a project without a second project to "test" that ability. In this sense, therefore, it is reasonable that the institution would have the training exercise and the test be the same thing. But it's a situation that creates some difficulty.

The "problem" with this test of managing and completing a project

Because the dissertation project is supposed to teach exactly those traits of self-management and self-guidance that it also tests, it creates something of a cart-before-the-horse problem in which a doctoral candidate can feel as if they're set up for failure because they have never learned or exercised the ability on which they're being tested. In my experience, this problem is not unusual; people struggle when they have to find a way where they have never gone before. Despite this very real problem, I would not condemn the dissertation project system as inherently problematic for a couple of reasons.

First, it is important to remember that the "dissertation project" is not a monolithic endeavor, but rather (as previously discussed) part of a larger research agenda made up of a web of interlocking questions, and it is a web of questions that you approach one day at a time, and each day, possibly, suggests a new path. It is a process of learning. Putting your ideas into words and actions and managing the overall project is itself a thing can only be learned through practice. You cannot learn to manage your own project without working on managing a project. You have to make the decisions yourself—you have to trust your judgment of how to proceed, and you have to be able to live with the consequences. Therefore, it is reasonable to expect you to learn as you go; the production of the dissertation is the evidence that you have learned these skills.

Secondly, as mentioned above, because it takes so long to design and carry out a research project, it makes sense to have the learning experience also be the test. There is no substitute for doing it yourself—no matter how many supervised exercises you are put through. But, as I said above, once you've completed your own project, it is sufficient proof that you have learned what was expected.

PROJECT INERTIA

As an aside: If you wonder how professors manage to publish several articles a year, despite the length of time it takes to set up a research study, just remember that each project is only one question in the larger research interest. The more time that you work on the larger research interest, the more potential research questions/research projects will appear. Over time, because it's more difficult to carry out an entire project than to do preliminary design, a scholar will develop a backlog of projects at different stages of development, and one publication can follow another closely because each successive project is already fairly mature at the time the preceding work goes to press.

This sort of project inertia won't help you finish your dissertation, but if you're aiming at an academic career, you may be able to get some projects started by leaving out some ideas that would be interesting additions to your dissertation, but that are excluded to limit its scope and finish it as quickly as possible. Instead of feeling like you're losing these insights each time you exclude something interesting from your dissertation, you see them as opportunities for future research and publication.

In short, you are being tested by the dissertation. Seeing the dimensions on which you are being tested, and recognizing that these dimensions relate to traits that will be beneficial to your future, can help you successfully pass the test of the dissertation.

CHAPTER 7.2
MANAGING PEOPLE, ESPECIALLY YOUR PROFESSORS

In practical terms, the institution manifests in the person of the professors (and perhaps other faculty/staff) who review your work. Therefore, central to fulfilling the institutional requirements is to fulfill the desires and expectations of those with whom you work and those who will review your work. Speaking pragmatically, and perhaps a bit cynically, you will benefit from thinking about what you want to get and how you can get it from the people with whom you work.

This last perspective to be discussed might be the most cynical, but it is eminently practical. One very basic way to look at the dissertation is this: if the right people sign it, it's a dissertation. What, then, can you do to get them to sign it? But in this practical view, it should be remembered that you can get more from your professors than just their signatures on the final document. Professors, after all, are supposed to teach you and help you! It's what they get paid for. It's reasonable to expect useful guidance and support from your professors. I know it's easy to find people with some horror story about being poorly treated by their professors, but I would guess that it's even easier to find students who are appreciative of all that they got from their professors.

A more complimentary way of framing this issue is to point out that you can benefit from carefully managing your interactions with the people with whom you work. And it is to your benefit to think about the nature of your interactions—especially with respect to feedback—in order to understand how to best manage them. Although the material here is very much directed at the question of working with professors on your dissertation committee, the basic principles are really transferable to almost any area: Wherever you deal with people, you will benefit from thinking about how to manage the interaction.

US VS. UK

The perspective discussed here is most relevant to the United States doctoral model. The biggest differences between the US and UK models lie in the different relationships between student and faculty. In the UK model, the supervisor with whom a student works is not the reviewer of the work, creating a very different dynamic than in the US, where there is greater incentive to cater to the interests of the committee. There are pros and cons to each model, but these differences will not be discussed at any length.

PROFESSORS ARE JUST PEOPLE

Maybe you've had your own difficulties with faculty. Chances are, you've heard about the troubles someone else had with someone on their faculty committee. Horror stories abound, and people may stretch the tales for dramatic purpose—I mentioned earlier how one book on dissertation writing likens graduated students who show appreciation for their professors to released kidnap victims suffering from Stockholm syndrome. Professors sometimes do bad things, it's undeniable. Professors have power over their students, and sometimes they abuse that power—just as others with power sometimes abuse their power. Some professors are just plain rotten people, and ought to be avoided, if at all possible.

On the other hand, some professors are really excellent, kind, moral people. And most of them are in between. Professors, after all, are just people, and in any group of people, you'll naturally find a range of characters. Ideally, you have an opportunity to get to know your professors a little, or at least get to know of them by reputation before you have to make a choice for your dissertation committee. Practically speaking, however, you'll be choosing among a small group of people—those in your department doing the same kind of work as you—if you get to choose at all. But even if you're working with the worst of the lot, your chances will be much better if you make good decisions about how to interact with them. Although the power dynamic between the student and professor is unequal, you should not believe that you, the student, have no power. You have a lot of power to choose how you approach the people with whom you work, and how you respond to them. Choose wisely, and your path will be easier (not easy, but much easier).

CREATING A POSITIVE IMPRESSION AND AVOIDING CONFLICT

You want to do things that will keep you out of your committee's doghouse. You want your committee to believe that you are capable, that you have acted responsibly, and that your work has similarly been responsibly developed and carried out. You can do this without any demeaning bootlicking (providing that your committee is not made up of ego-tripping psychopaths). There are, I think, five key points:

- You want to avoid emotional conflicts.

- You want to accept their recommendations whenever reasonable or possible, if for no other reason than to give them a sense of power. And if you have reservations about a suggestion, you want to be able to state those reservations clearly.

- You want to ask them to look at a reasonable amount of your work; you don't want to drown them in it.

- Learn how to ask for feedback.

- Learn how to use feedback productively.

These points may seem obvious, but they're key components to success.

Avoiding emotional conflicts

The first point is, in a way, the most challenging: you can't control the emotional antics of your professors (and, sadly, sometimes they can't either, which is often the source of the problem). If you get lucky, there will be no antics, but figuring out how to guide a path through the thickets of academia is difficult, even with good professors. Chances for emotional conflict are greater if you are closely involved with your committee members in areas outside of your dissertation work.

As I said, professors are people, and they are prone to the variations that all people are prone to. Not all professors are emotionally mature, honest, or altruistic. And not all professors are selfish, self-centered, and abusive. It is to be hoped that your professors are good people, but regardless of who they are, you want to make plans that lead to your success. You don't want to turn your dissertation into a battle with professors and administrators; you want to get the powers that be to serve you as much as possible. In an ideal world, you would be able to get your professors to be actively supportive; many professors will be. It might not be possible to avoid conflicts, but if you work to avoid such conflicts, you may be able to avoid trouble.

You want your professors to focus on the work that you're doing; conflicts of any sort, even theoretical, can lead to emotional responses that take attention away from the research concerns. This is not to suggest that you should abandon your own theoretical commitments in order to please your professors. Some professors are happy to work with theories that they do not themselves accept. Unfortunately, some professors are limited by their own beliefs. There is no simple answer to dealing with a professor who says "This doesn't agree with what I believe."[42] It would be better to work with someone more supportive and more open to your own ideas, but sometimes it isn't feasible or possible to find someone else to work with.

As a general rule, you can promote amity with others by agreeing with them. One of the key routes for developing a good relationship between you and your professors is to take their recommendations seriously.

---

42   I wish I had a better answer to resolving real theoretical conflicts than saying that, in the end, if your professor is completely closed to an idea you hold, you might have to abandon that idea, regardless of the support that idea may have in the general population. If you believe in TheoryX and your professor absolutely rejects it and any work that depends on it, then you either need to abandon TheoryX or you need to find another professor.

Taking recommendations and refusing recommendations

Everyone likes to feel like they have useful things to say. People in positions of power—like your professors—like to have useful things to say—and they often do; they also like to be respected, and may even want to be obeyed, thinking that their position of power was awarded because of their experience and good judgment. For these reasons, accepting their advice generally creates in them a predisposition to like you and think you're smart. They think they're smart; they think their advice is good. Therefore they also usually think that it's smart for you to take their advice, and so taking their advice may well be taken as a sign of your general intelligence.

And professors often do have good advice. They have succeeded in their field, and the wisdom they have gained might well help you move forward. You should seriously consider the possibility that your professors' advice is based on wisdom.

This is not to recommend becoming a slave to a professor. The point of the doctoral dissertation is to show that you are an independent scholar, so you shouldn't let your independence slip away. If there is something that you think is wrong with a professor's recommendation, then you need to examine that and understand it. If, on examination, you still feel it is an important difference of opinion, you need to be willing to present the argument to your professor.

As stated by the previous principle: you don't want to create emotional conflicts. So you want to make sure that the differences that you express with them are not motivated by emotional resistance, and you want to make sure that when you express differences to them, you do so in a way that avoids triggering an emotional response, which means developing clear, well-reasoned explanations for any differences that you wish to express. Sometimes logic and emotion will conflict—if, for example, you have decided that there are logical flaws in the main theory that your professor espouses, you may want to avoid that battle: there will be emotional links to ideas a person supports, so even a logical explanation of differences may cause problems. On the other hand, if there is some specific aspect of difference within a larger framework of agreement, you have a good chance of explaining the difference as a matter of logic and reason that doesn't trigger negative emotional responses, and may trigger some positive ones. Right or wrong, if you have carefully thought through and presented an argument in favor of something, that speaks in your favor as an independent scholar.

In short: choose your battles, and try to follow suggestions unless the circumstances really warrant debate.

Give professors the right amount of work

You want your professors to think of you as a productive scholar. You want to get their feedback. You don't want to annoy them. To accomplish this you want to give them the right amount of the right kind of work.

This is something of a balancing act: you want to find the amount of work that they will respond to well, and this is dependent on their expectations. A preliminary step to discovering what they would consider the right amount of work is to ask them—not necessarily "how much work should I turn in?", but you can certainly ask them what they feel like a good scope for a piece of work is, and use that as a guideline. You can ask them how long they expect pieces to take to write, and take that into account as you make your plans and schedules. You should, of course, set your pace to suit your abilities, but by understanding your professors' expectations and desires, you can do a better job of giving them things that please them, and this is not to be scorned. Asking to understand a professor's expectations does not condemn you to doing what they expect. It does give you information that can be put to good use in planning your efforts.

However much work you decide to turn in, you can do two things to keep the quantity of work from bothering your professors:

- Try to turn in amounts of work according to their schedule and expectations, and

- Make sure that you are really making changes: Don't just send them a revised paragraph every day (unless they asked for it), and especially don't send them a complete draft in which only one or two paragraphs are different—at least not without clearly marking the changes that have been made.

It is very important to avoid wasting people's time, especially your professors', because they're very busy (as a general principle, it's good to treat others' time as valuable). Your professors' attention is a resource that can avail you, but it's limited, so use it wisely. Your professors surely see their time as a valuable resource, so don't do things that lead them to think that you're wasting it.

Ideally, each successive draft that you give a professor will show a significant response to the feedback they gave you previously, and also significant development on your part as well. This will help keep professors from getting bored with the tedium of looking for minor changes in a large work, thereby limiting their resentment of the work of looking through your writing.

Learn how to ask for feedback

If you ask good questions, you'll get good answers. You can send your draft to your professors and say, "Here's the new one; what do you think?" That will work very well in some situations—especially if you have made major revisions or you have been in communication with them about the changes that you have been working on. But generally speaking, you're going to get better feedback if you prime your readers to attend to the things that you care about. Tell them what you want them to look at and you'll get more useful feedback.

Perhaps the most important part of this is trying to get feedback appropriate to your stage in the process: if you're trying to get the main ideas worked out, then you want to direct your professors' attention to the main ideas and steer them away from things like formatting and grammar. If this seems obvious to you, good! Remember it! I have worked with many writers who, on turning in an early draft of a dissertation while they were still trying to get their central ideas in order, received feedback on their sentence structure, formatting, etc. The feedback, therefore, didn't help them move forward, because it did not address issues related to the main story. I'm not excusing sloppy work, or saying that you should turn in sloppy work. To expect anyone—including your professors—to wade through a complete mess is silly. But if your work is messy but readable and you haven't fully worked out the research questions, then you want to get feedback on the research questions, not on your punctuation or citation style.

Be explicit in telling people how they can help you. Give them instructions on what to look for. Submit your work with a cover letter that says, "I know that I need to clean up the writing, but could you please focus on the following issues: . . . ?" Or, "I've been trying to resolve the following issues: . . . I'm sorry it's a bit of a mess; I know I have to clean that up." If you haven't fully edited, warn your reader that you are aware of the need to fix punctuation, citations, and the rest, and tell them that they need not worry about such issues because you plan on taking care of them. Provide a detailed list of concerns—especially in early drafts—so that your readers focus on the things that matter to you. If you give them a cover letter asking them to focus on specific issues, they're far less likely to give you feedback on an issue that isn't of interest to you. (And, as an aside, tying to write that cover letter will be a useful exercise in trying to express your main points.) Sometimes it's interesting to give people a work without guidance to see what their response is, but if you want directed feedback, ask for it. Don't just hope that you'll get good feedback; take active steps to improve the quality of the feedback you receive.

USING FEEDBACK

To get the most out of feedback, you want to respond as un-emotionally as possible. Step back from your work and consider the quality of the feedback and try to understand what you can get out of it. Not all feedback is equal.

Some will help; some will not. Some is appropriate; some is not. Being able to recognize which is which, and what to do with what you got, are valuable skills. This is one aspect to trusting yourself: be willing to evaluate the quality of the feedback you receive. The feedback you get reveals how someone responded, which is a combination of their own issues and the issues present in the draft that you submit.

Central to using any feedback is to distance yourself from your work, and to distance your work from their feedback. You want to respond in a fashion as objective and analytical as possible. At the very least, you don't want to let an emotional response of anger or dismay lead you into imprudent action. If the responses you got are unpleasant, try not to focus on how you've been misunderstood, instead focus on the question of how to change your paper so that you get better responses in the future.

The first level of distancing is to remember that your project is a work in progress, and flaws in the project are not reflections of your ability, but merely roughnesses in the project. There is a reason editors exist, after all: even the best writers benefit from help. If the work you have created has problems or is rough, you can fix it or get it fixed!

The second level of distancing is to remember that audience response is not just a product of the work but also of the audience. Great works have been rejected by audiences. Sometimes rejection is due to the blindness of the reviewer, not the failure of the creator. There are any number of failures of an audience, many of which can be alleviated by a good cover letter, as mentioned above. But regardless of the cover letter you might have sent, the feedback you get might be of poor quality due to the reader. Maybe they were busy, maybe distracted, maybe grumpy or ill. Regardless of who made the feedback, you can always ask: "Is this feedback suitable to the work? Does this feedback address important issues?" Trust yourself to judge the feedback you get. Not all feedback will be useful, and if you don't get in the habit of testing the worth of comments, you will be at the mercy of bad feedback.

People make mistakes; some feedback is just plain wrong. You have to be willing to challenge obvious errors. Other times, the feedback isn't wrong, but it is off-base. I worked with a writer who was trying to feel out the main theme of her dissertation when she offered a first version of a chapter draft to her advisor. The feedback that she got was a few comments on sentence structure, which led her to focus her attention on sentences of that sort, which led to her spending a couple of frustrating days trying to rewrite a draft only to discover that she was still faced with the same concerns of trying to find her story. A more confident writer might have looked at the same feedback and said "sure, but that's not my concern now." And in such a case, a writer might decide to make a more specific request for feedback, saying something like, "Yes, I appreciate your suggestions about the sentence structure. Thank you. I was also wondering about these issues, . . . and I had questions about . . ." Responding to feedback gives you an opportunity to please your professors: you say to them, "See how these changes incorporate the suggestions and corrections you have made?"

SUMMARY

Your dissertation depends on your getting the signatures of your committee (and possibly of other administrators), and you benefit from having their help and support. It's a lot easier to finish a dissertation if you have your committee's active support; it's a lot harder to finish if there is conflict between you. Although, speaking abstractly, you have the right to be treated well by your committee, professors are people, with all the faults and foibles of people. You're going to make better progress by working to manage, develop, and strengthen your relationship with your committee in the ways you can, rather than in complaining about what they are doing wrong. This is not to say that you should accept abuse, but rather to say that you should look to prevent or avoid it through your own actions. In addition, because professors are busy people, part of developing a good relationship with them and getting the most of your relationship with them is making reasonable requests of them, and then using their suggestions when possible and appropriate.

CONCLUSION

Ultimately, I believe that almost everybody who has started a dissertation will be best served by finishing the dissertation as soon as possible and then getting on with the rest of their life. By closing the door on your dissertation—even if it is imperfect—you will open new doors, doors that you may have been aiming at for years! So step back from the task for a moment. Take the time to look at it from different angles, and make some plans for effective action to bring it all to a beneficial conclusion.

Many writers find that their dissertation becomes a weight dragging them down. The problem is serious enough that people write books talking abut surviving dissertations. Academia is a publish-or-perish world; if you can't get your dissertation done and accepted, then your academic career is likely to perish. If you're aiming for a professional career that needs a doctorate, you're similarly in need of finishing your dissertation.

A dissertation, despite all the hard work and likely frustrations, need not be an unrewarding burden. It is an opportunity, too.

The dissertation can be viewed in many different lights and angles. If you view it too often in just one light, it is easier to become stuck and to lose sight of (and even lose out on) many of the benefits that would be available. By having a variety of perspectives, you can better see different avenues of action that will help you move toward completion. If you can see the dissertation from different angles, you are in a better position to respond to difficulties, avoid getting trapped, and ultimately get the benefits you have been seeking.

The perspectives that I have outlined in this book are all important in turning your dissertation project into a productive and beneficial experience. These perspectives focus on aspects of the dissertation that can influence your performance—from the importance of good health to the importance of recognizing the dynamics of the larger research processes of individuals and institutions to the importance of the personal relationships that impinge on your work. By having all these perspectives at your disposal, you can plan a more effective and efficient course through the difficulties of the work, so that some day soon you will have gotten the best of your dissertation.

REFERENCES

Belcher, W. L. (2009). *Writing Your Journal Article in 12 Weeks: A Guide to Academic Publishing Success.* Thousand Oaks, CA: Sage.

Boice, R. (1990). *Professors as Writers: A Self-Help Guide to Productive Writing.* Stillwater, OK: New Forums Press.

Bolker, J. (ed.) (1997). *The Writer's Home Companion.* New York: Owl Books.

Booth, W. C., Colomb, G. G., & Williams, J. M. (2008). *The Craft of Research* (3rd. edition). Chicago, IL: University of Chicago Press.

Csikszentmihalyi, M. (1991). *Flow: The Psychology of Optimal Experience.* New York, NY: Harper Perennial.

Fiore, N. (1989). *The Now Habit.* Los Angeles, CA: Tarcher.

Foucault, M. (1971/1994). *The Order of Things.* New York, NY: Vintage. [Reprint of 1971 Pantheon translation of *Les Mots et les Choses,* 1966.]

Frankl, V. (1959/1984). *Man's Search For Meaning.* New York, NY: Washington Square Press.

Graff, G., & Berkenstein, C. (2007). *They Say/I Say.* New York, NY: Norton.

Hjortshoj, K. (2001). *Understanding Writing Blocks.* New York, NY: Oxford University Press.

Kahneman, D. (2011). *Thinking, Fast and Slow.* New York, NY: Farrar, Strauss and Giroux.

Kuhn, T. (1970). *The Structure of Scientific Revolutions* (Second Edition, enlarged). Chicago, IL: University of Chicago Press.

Lamott, A. (1994). *Bird by Bird*. New York, NY: Anchor Books.

Latour, B. (1987). S*cience in Action: How to Follow Scientists and Engineers Through Society*. Cambridge, MA: Harvard University Press.

Lovitts, B., (2007). *Making the Implicit Explicit*. Sterling, VA: Stylus.

Popper, K. (1959). *The Logic of Scientific Discovery*. [Originally published in German as Logik der Forschung, 1935.]

Popper, K. (1979). *Objective Knowledge: An Evolutionary Approach* (revised edition). New York: Oxford University Press.

Protzen, J.-P., & Harris, D. J. (2010). *The Universe of Design: Horst Rittel's Theories of Design and Planning*. London, UK: Routledge.

Rudestam, K. E., & Newton, R. R. (2007). *Surviving Your Dissertation: A Comprehensive Guide to Content and Process*. Los Angeles, CA: Sage.

Russell, B. (1918/1985). *The Philosophy of Logical Atomism*. La Salle, IL: Open Court.

Servan-Schreiber, D. (2004). *The Instinct to Heal*. Emmaus, PA: Rodale.

Single, P. B. (2009). *Demystifying Dissertation Writing*. Sterling, VA: Stylus.

Sternberg, D. (1981). *How to Complete and Survive a Doctoral Dissertation*. New York, NY: St. Martin's Press.

Turner, M. (1996). *The Literary Mind*. New York, NY: Oxford University Press.

Wright, R. O. (1990). *A Little Bit at a Time: Secrets of Productive Quality*. Berkeley, CA: Ten Speed Press.

Zerubavel, E. (1999). *The Clockwork Muse: A Practical Guide to Writing Theses, Dissertations, and Books*. Cambridge, MA: Harvard University Press.

ABOUT THE AUTHOR

Dave Harris has been working as an editor and academic writing coach since 2002, the year he finished his own Ph.D. at the University of California, Berkeley. After reading a lot of dissertation books he decided to write his own because none of the ones he read looked at the dissertation from the perspectives that have been successful with his clients.

WWW.THOUGHTCLEARING.COM

Made in the USA
Columbia, SC
23 May 2018